THE COMPETITIVE ADVANTAGES OF
FAR EASTERN BUSINESS

The Competitive Advantages of Far Eastern Business

Edited by

ROBERT FITZGERALD

International Monetary Fund
Joint Library

2 5 1995

International Bank for
Reconstruction and Development
Washington, D.C. 20431

FRANK CASS

First published in 1994 in Great Britain by
FRANK CASS AND COMPANY LIMITED
Newbury House, 890–900 Eastern Avenue,
Newbury Park, Ilford, Essex IG2 7HH

and in the United States of America by
FRANK CASS
c/o International Specialized Book Services, Inc.
5602 N.E. Hassalo Street, Portland, Oregon 927213-3640

Copyright © 1994 Frank Cass & Co. Ltd.

British Library Cataloguing in Publication Data

Comparative Advantages of Far Eastern
Business. – (Studies in Far Eastern
Business, ISSN 1351-0363)
 I. Fitzgerald, Robert II. Series
338.095

ISBN 0-7146-4592-3 (cased) ISBN 0-7146-4144-8 (paper)

Library of Congress Cataloging-in-Publication Data

The Comparative advantages of Far Eastern business / edited by Robert Fitzgerald.
   p. cm.—(Studies in Far Eastern business, ISSN 1351-0363)
   "This group of studies first appeared in a special issue of the Journal of Far Eastern Business, Vol.1, No.1., Autumn 1994"—T.p. verso.
   Includes bibliographical references.
   ISBN 0-7146-4592-3 (cased) ISBN 0-7146-4144-8 (paper)
   1. Industrial promotion—East Asia. 2. East Asia—Industries.
3. East Asia—Economic conditions. I. Series.
HC460.5.C63 1994
332.6'73225—dc20   94-10026
                                                                    CIP

This group of studies first appeared in a Special Issue of the
Journal of Far Eastern Business (Vol.1, No.1 Autumn 1994),
[*The Competitive Advantages of Far Eastern Business*].

*All rights reserved. No part of this publication may be reproduced,
stored in a retrieval system, or transmitted in any form, or by any
means, electronic, mechanical, photocopying, recording or otherwise
without the prior permission of Frank Cass and Company Limited.*

Typeset by Vitaset, Paddock Wood, Kent
Printed in Great Britain by Antony Rowe, Chippenham, Wilts

Contents

Comparisons and Explanations of National
   Economic Success: Analysing East Asia   ROBERT FITZGERALD   1

A Dynamic Approach to International
   Competitiveness: The Case of Korea   DONG-SUNG CHO   17

The Competitive Advantage of Japanese
   Industries: Developments, Dimensions and
   Directions   YOSHITAKA SUZUKI   37

Trade, Industry and Government: The
   Development of Organisational Capabilities
   in Singapore   SIOW-YUE CHIA   52

Competitive Advantage in the Context of
   Hong Kong   S.G. REDDING   71

The Competitive Advantage of Taiwan   LAWRENCE J. LAU   90

Comparisons and Explanations of National Economic Success: Analysing East Asia

ROBERT FITZGERALD

The speed of economic growth in East Asia has conjured up a range of resonant descriptions, from national 'Tigers' to regional 'Miracle' and imminent 'Pacific Century'. The rise of Japan as a post-war superpower has been paralleled by the success of South Korea, Taiwan, Singapore and Hong Kong, the collective 'Four Tigers', and by the newly-emergent countries of Malaysia, Thailand and Indonesia. The rate of respective GDP change over many years, culminating in an industrial and trading region of world importance, has been seen as a phenomenon of unprecedented or, more dramatically, 'miraculous' proportions. Prospects are enhanced by the rapid expansion of mainland China, the giant of East Asia, and by the strengthening of ties with America and Australasia, and countries within and outside the Pacific Basin have been weighing the long-term economic and strategic implications. The value of goods transversing the Pacific now surpasses the worth of the Atlantic trade, and the global economy is rightly viewed as a system of dominant regions in North America, western Europe and the Far East. Given this evolving triangulation, it is too early to project the circumstance of a 'Pacific Century', and the term 'miracle' can be misleading if it suggests unique, almost inexplicable occurrences. The leading Far Eastern nations do stand as object lessons in development economics, but entrenched and widespread industrialisation from a position of recent, comparative disadvantage is understandable in terms that give full credit to the hard-won fruits of human and capital accumulation.

It is possible to distinguish rates and patterns of economic growth in specific Far Eastern nations which possess common characteristics, and their interdependence, driven on by Japanese foreign direct investment and a shared commitment to export-orientated industrialisation, encourages convergence. The causes of rapid development can be enumerated, and they might include cultural attributes, government policy, and competitive markets, in addition to high savings ratios and committed investment in education, production facilities and technology. It is questionable, and certainly difficult to decide, whether these all-embracing factors have more similarities than dissimilarities in their specific contribution to economic growth in each case. The World Bank report on *The East Asian Miracle* is correct in identifying and isolating the

---

Robert Fitzgerald, Royal Holloway, University of London

eight 'High Performing Asian Economies' of Japan, the Four Tigers and newly industrialising Malaysia, Thailand and Indonesia, because they share remarkable growth rates as well as geographical proximity. They all find a place amongst those 20 countries which achieved the highest change in per capita GDP between 1960 and 1985, and six of them can be found amongst the first seven. During this period, average real income in Japan, Korea, Taiwan, Singapore and Hong Kong has more than quadrupled, and living standards have more than doubled in the South East Asian NICs. Overall, these eight economies have between 1965 and 1990 grown on a per capita basis twice as fast as either the OECD membership or the rest of Asia, and comparisons with Latin America, South Asia and Sub-Saharan Africa are even more noteworthy. One striking feature is the mixture of high growth rates and declining inequality.[1] They have fulfilled, therefore, Kuznets' criteria for *modern economic growth*: these societies have been or are being transformed by the application of technology in industrial production, and rises in average measures of real per capita income have taken place over a long period and directly benefited the majority of people.[2] It is the compounded effect of growth from the 1960s onwards and over several decades which has marked out the Far East, especially when so many advanced nations have achieved only very modest annual increases in GDP.

TABLE 1
ASIA PACIFIC ECONOMIC COOPERATION STATISTICS

	1991 GDP $bn	1991 GNP per head $	GNP Growth per head 1980-91 % p.a.	Export Volume Growth 1980-91 % p.a.
East Asia & Pacific	961,754	650	6.1	10.2
US	5,610,800	22,240	1.7	4.0
Japan	3,362,300	26,930	3.6	3.9
World	21,639,100	4,010	1.2	4.1

Source: World Bank, *Global Economic Prospects and the Developing Countries* (1993).

Although the fact of rapid economic development can be traced, it is no surprise that interpretations of the root causes do not enjoy broad consensus. In fact, there are very few comparative works on the economies of the Far East, and, despite a burgeoning literature on individual nations, there is an unmet demand for research which systematically examines the determinants of growth and rising living standards throughout the region. The World Bank's report and its many supporting commissioned papers have attracted attention precisely because of the breadth of its data. It concentrates on the actions of governments, and argues that the successful Far Eastern nations have attended to 'basics' by maintaining 'sound' macroeconomic policies, low inflation and financial rectitude. The report does affirm the ways in which public policy has encouraged competitive business and trading environments, high savings ratios, and human skills and capital accumulation. Variations in experience are admitted, but, while the existence of an efficient civil service and a willingness to raise educational standards are admitted, the state is not accorded a leading role. The World Bank has produced a considered report that traces the economic history and circumstances of each country, and, in recognising problems of interpretation, it partially concedes the validity of other viewpoints. Its conclusions have not been free of criticism, mainly because they are predicated upon a neo-classical perspective. By acknowledging state activism to be important in the early stages of economic development, the World Bank accepts the benefits of 'market-friendly' government policies, but, as one would expect from its source, the report is in the final analysis heavily market-orientated in its emphasis.[3]

The achievement of economic development and transformation in the Far Eastern economies is open to varieties of alternative analysis, and they all have the same ability to match the available facts. The belief that less advanced nations cannot depend on markets precisely because these mechanisms are ill-developed is well established.[4] The process of industrialisation in many west European and East Asian countries over the last 100 years may contain elements that differentiate them from the more protracted Anglo-American experience, potentially a better match for the views of the World Bank. The dynamic economies of the Far East are self-evidently driven by private sector enterprise, but both governments and businesses have adopted pragmatic, flexible strategies which on many occasions have accepted the need for state activism and inter-company cooperation. Price 'distortions', credit and capital controls, taxation incentives, and selective import barriers have been used as instruments of industrial policies shaped by a mixture of economic, strategic and defence considerations.[5] Governments have been determined to nurture and found leading sectors which can ultimately compete with companies from advanced industrial nations, create value-added, and raise living standards. What may distinguish the successful Far Eastern economies from their neighbours and other developing nations is that these policies have not been entirely government-directed but dependent on the establishment of consensus, the involvement of business leaders, and the cultivated support of the populace. Far Eastern companies generally compete fiercely for markets, but they have greater inclination and opportunity for cooperation, most notably within enterprise groups like the Japanese *keiretsu*, through holding company structures like the Korean *chaebol*, or as a result of the small-scale family enterprises typical of Chinese societies. These connections reflect in part the need for rapid growth out of relative backwardness. Undeveloped capital markets have necessitated close bank–industry relations or the sourcing of funds through extended cousinage. Governments may also influence the flow of domestic and foreign capital, as well as the licensing and importation of foreign technology. Buyer–supplier linkages and distribution networks are often organised on the same long-term, reciprocal basis as bank–industry relations, and an initial lack of technical knowledge, a shortage of managerial personnel, inexperience of product and export markets, and a dearth of funds may induce expanding companies in newly emergent nations to pool resources. Within Chinese businesses, small-scale, labour-intensive and flexible manufacturing strategies as well as personal and affiliational relationships bolster cooperative arrangements. In short, 'market substitutes' in the form of government agencies or private sector associations and groups may be critical whenever the market and open competition provide too many obstacles to desired development goals, or, alternatively, merely offer the prospect of exposure to overwhelming foreign competition. Transforming nations have to create economic institutions which efficiently allocate capital, promote research and development, and establish infrastructure, in addition to increasing productivity, investing in human resources, regulating and encouraging competition, and maintaining a degree of social welfare. The desired mixture of state, intercompany cooperation, and market may vary between industries, countries and stages of economic development, and changes in attitudes and methods of operations are apparent in several cases. Within Japan, the role of the Ministry of International Trade and Industry and the *keiretsu* groups, important in the immediate post-war years, appears to have decreased in relation to individual concerns.

The World Bank report is located in a macroeconomic as well as a neoclassical form of analysis, and this approach often overlooks the very existence of government agencies, large-scale companies and other institutions, which can from a theoretical point of view 'distort' the workings of 'perfectly competitive markets'.[6] Cautious fiscal policies may be a feature of Far Eastern countries, yet economic transformation and industrialisation have been the product of institution-building. Transforming or advanced economies function through a complex network of human institutions and organisations, and the interactions of both private companies and governmental bodies can enhance productive efficiency and public support for economic objectives. The World Bank report does discuss the 'institutional basis' of growth: it explores the evolution of educational provision, reputable civil services, state-business development councils, savings and lending institutions, infrastructure, and export capability as means of increasing productive capacity, and the implementation of land reform and the availability of housing and public health services as techniques for sharing wealth.[7] But, despite these discursions, the report concentrates on issues of political economy, and its emphasis remains predominantly macroeconomic. Any investigation that goes beyond the World Bank's interest in public policy might adopt a more microèconomic approach and focus instead on businesses, management and organisational forms. As the successful East Asian countries are free market economies, it has largely been private sector companies, with the assistance of governments and the natural and created factor endowments to be found in each nation, that have been the engines of growth. In the development of institutions which can modernise, transform and become a vital component of economically efficient systems – containing both competitive and cooperative elements – it is no surprise to say that success has rested on companies and industries acquiring organisational capabilities and winning products.

It is Michael Porter who has explicitly linked micro- and meso-level strengths and competencies with the economic fortunes of nations. He seeks to explain why certain companies and industries have grown in some countries and not in others, and why certain economies have expanded in recent decades while others have stagnated or declined. In *Competitive Strategy*, published in 1980, he dealt with matters of industrial structure, competitor behaviour and the formulation of corporate strategy. Successful firms, he contended, have to guard against the activities of existing rivals, buyers, suppliers, new entrants, and potential providers of substitute products, and they must acquire a position within each industry where they gain the greatest profits from the value-added. They must also adopt strategies of price competitiveness, product differentiation, or the application of either in specialist markets, and so gain an advantage over rivals and an effective barrier against market entry.[8] Porter's work was distinguished by a rigorous theoretical framework and detailed investigation of various competitive scenarios, and, within business schools and amongst management executives, it benefited from its seeming ability to reflect real life situations, a feeling assisted by the plethora of illustrative case studies. Porter's reputation was enhanced by *Competitive Advantage*, which was issued in 1985, expounded further on the three strategies of price, differentiation and focus, and discussed the sustaining of commercial leadership. His description of the value-chain was a useful conceptual advance. All firms engage in the primary activities of inbound logistics, operations, outbound logistics, marketing and sales, and in the supporting activities of planning, finance, human resource management, technological upgrading, and procurement. Each is a sum of all these activities, and, whenever a firm performs these activities better than its competitors, it gains a competitive advantage. Through efficient management, it can win cost-leadership; by adding higher value for buyers, it can create premium-price products. In any profitable firm, it follows that the cost of primary and secondary activities is less than the value of its output, and long-term success requires the creation and maintenance of organisational capabilities, whether they are human, technical, financial or physical.[9]

In *The Competitive Advantage of Nations*, published in 1990, Porter moves from his explanations of individual company performance to the more difficult and ambitious analysis of national economic success. By building upon his corpus of established work, he seeks to establish the mainsprings of macroeconomic achievement at the level of the industry and its component firms, and, to fulfil his objectives, he engages in the art of international comparison. Alfred Chandler's *Scale and Scope* possesses obvious parallels with Porter's *Competitive Advantage of Nations*: coincidentally released in the same year, its intellectual roots can be found in previous books, and it shares a comparative perspective and an insistence on a micro- or meso-economic analysis. Chandler's historical survey has been a major and widely acknowledged contribution to the study of business, but its evidence terminates in the 1950s, covers only three countries, and concentrates on the rise of multidivisional, industrial corporations. While his book benefits from the *depth* (or, if preferred, *scale*) of research, Porter's analysis has the advantage of *breadth* (or *scope*). As a result, Chandler's path-breaking study does not have the applicability that is evident in Porter's schema.[10] In *The Competitive Advantage of Nations*, Porter begins with his now familiar outline of industrial structure, strategy, and the gaining and maintenance of competitive advantage through price, product differentiation or market focus. He also develops his ideas on the value-chain. It is theoretically possible for firms to undertake almost all the process stages and support activities which are needed to supply a good or service, but it is not seen as an essential prerequisite of success.[11] Chandler would probably accept the notion that the boundaries formed between the internalisation of activities within companies and reliance on the market mechanism differ according to the varying influence of transaction costs in specific industries. Yet his work has focused on the rise of the modern industrial corporations in certain sectors, at a time when technological and marketing advantages lay with increasing returns to scale and the 'visible hand' of managerial direction. Porter is uninterested in prescriptive preferences for either small-scale or large-scale organisation, and debates on the replacement of the Chandlerian managerial hierarchy by flatter, more flexible organisational structures are generally overlooked.[12] Porter believes that there are a range of viable choices and that these are determined by a multitude of contingencies.

He is concerned with the dependence of competitive advantage and profitability on the existence of efficiently organised value-chains, and, while some national industries may be dominated by corporations, others may function through effective market coordination and reciprocal, interfirm linkages. Indeed, the very existence of a successful company will encourage the rival firms, buyers, suppliers, finishers, and banking, transport and other services, and, finally, the emergence of whole sectors with product affinities or sectors with the type of connections that link steel, shipbuilding, cars, and machine tools in Japan. The development of these national industrial clusters, often regionally located, has a mutually beneficial and self-reinforcing influence on the competitive advantages of the industries concerned, providing them with an available pool of organisational capability, resources and expertise with which to win world markets. It is the management and development of the value-chain which establishes the relationship between firm-level competitiveness and the rise of whole industries, and the economic fortunes and competitive advantage of nations rest upon the existence and meso-level capabilities of industrial clusters within each country. At this point, Porter can address the question of why certain industries have been able to gain globally competitive advantages in particular nations but not in others. The existence, success and competitive advantages of industrial clusters are shaped by international variations in the four components of national business environments (see Figure 1).

FIGURE 1

PORTER'S DETERMINANTS OF NATIONAL COMPETITIVE ADVANTAGE: THE DIAMOND

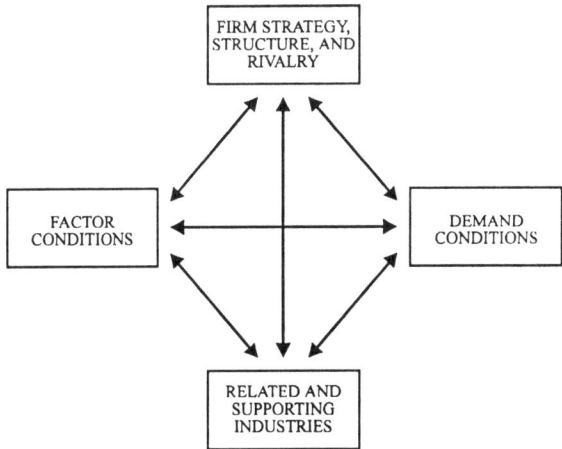

- *factor conditions* include created factor endowments such as human skill, knowledge, technology, and infrastructure, and natural factor endowments like arable land, geographical location, and energy and mineral resources;

- *demand conditions* are equated with the specific demand needs of each country, the absolute level of demand, and qualitative considerations such as the sophistication and expectations of consumers;

- *firm strategy, structure and rivalry* assesses the goals, industrial organisation and levels of rivalry within a nation and a specific industry, and the ways in which these can contribute or detract from competitive success;

- *related and supporting industries* with both vertical linkages along the many process stages and affinities in products, technology, production systems and marketing have an important impact on the capabilities of every sector.

All of these factors influence and interreact with each other, and national differences in each of these elements promote the growth of particular industrial clusters over others. Just as numerous and related clusters exploiting the advantages of their business environment are contributing to the national success of Japan and other Far Eastern economies, Britain is experiencing the long-term decline of whole industries and the associated unravelling of its economic base. Porter then lists some additional factors. Governments have a bearing on educational provision, research and development, infrastructural investment, and the promotion of competition, but he sees their proper role as supportive and partial. Given the impossibility of including every historical occurrence in a theoretical framework, he adds the contribution of chance events to the development of national industries. Like government, however, this consideration can be seen as a peripheral factor. Porter places inputs, demand conditions, related industries, and strategy and stucture in a diagram where they compose the four inter-connected points of his 'diamond' (see enclosed representation). This forms Porter's main conceptual tool, precisely because it links economic success, growth, and the pattern of global rivalry with national conditions and the founding of specific industrial clusters.[13]

Finally, Porter explores the competitive development of national economies. He argues that countries progress by upgrading their competitive positions, through the achievement of higher order advantages in existing industries and the development of capabilities in new, high-productivity segments and industries. The process requires a loss of position in price-sensitive segments and in products requiring less sophisticated skills and technology, which can be more effectively made overseas in less advanced countries. Porter seeks to identify predominant trends in the industrial activities of nations at different stages of development. He acknowledges that these discerned trends are generalisations; it is not axiomatic for every country to go through each of his stated stages, especially the last; and a decline in productivity and competitiveness is as likely as the desired process of upgrading. Each of the stages is associated with the determinants of national competitive advantage which are described within the 'diamond'. Accordingly, nations at the factor-driven stage contain internationally successful industries that draw their advantage almost solely from basic factors of production, such as natural resources or a readily available, semi-skilled labour pool. As indigenous firms compete on price and use low-level technology, the range of industries and industry segments is greatly constrained. Porter believes that resource-poor nations like Japan and Korea – and presumably Taiwan, Singapore, and Hong Kong – first gain international success in labour-intensive, final consumer goods such as textiles or basic electronics. Singapore, moreover, is located within the factor-driven stage, because it is a production base for foreign multinationals that have been attracted by advantageous factor conditions, namely a low-cost, well-educated workforce and good infrastructure. It follows that upgrading beyond that already achieved will be capped until Singapore becomes a home-base for internationally competitive industries. At the investment-driven stage, firms construct modern, efficient and often large-scale facilities, which they equip with the best technology to be bought in international markets. Work skills are enhanced alongside product quality and processes, and factor conditions and firm strategy, structure and rivalry are the major forces of national competitive advantage. Industries continue to be geared for export markets or import substitution, but those which emerge as particularly successful do gain strength from domestic demand conditions. Porter believes that governments do possess a key role during the investment stage, through the protection of inchoate industries, the channelling of capital and scarce resources, and the encouragement of risk-taking and technology acquisition. Progress depends, too, on a consensus that allows the deferment of consumption for long-term benefit, and both Japan and Korea have illustrated broad support for the objectives of economic development.

Porter holds that Taiwan has passed through the factor-driven stage, and that it shows signs of completing subsequent steps in investment (see Lau in this volume). Korea, he contends, achieved the factor-driven stage in the 1950s, and, in the 1980s, it became increasingly investment-driven. Unlike their counterparts in Singapore, the government and business leaders of Korea adopted the riskier strategy of encouraging indigenous industries, and low labour costs and readily acquired technologies have helped their international companies achieve success in price-sensitive markets. While Taiwan's industries have similar inherent strengths, its companies do not have the international presence and organisational capabilities of the Korean *chaebol*. The full 'diamond' is in place for the innovation-driven stage: a nation competes through a broad range of industries; as incomes rise, domestic consumer demand becomes sophisticated; related industrial clusters are formed; and companies implement global strategies. Above all, the economy depends less on natural factor endowments and more on created opportunities in human resources, research and development, and other forms of organisational capability. Price-sensitive products are replaced by those enjoying higher productivity, greater differentiation, and measures of stable demand. Within East Asia, Porter asserts that only Japan, in the 1970s, has fulfilled the innovation stage. Japan is characterised by its systemic management of the value chain in many industries, and by the possession of industrial clusters making high-value products. In Porter's developmental model, there is an evident connection between the innovation-driven stage, the formation of clusters, and a commitment to product differentiation, and Japan is used as an epitome of successful development and firmly entrenched national competitive advantages. Countries reach a point of malaise at the wealth-driven stage, and competitiveness ebbs as dependency on acquired wealth, investments, and mature industries grows. Consumption has prevalence over investment and innovation; the determinants of national advantage within the 'diamond' unravel; and industrial clusters atrophy. Britain is selected for the dubious honour of being uniquely representative of this category.[14]

To what extent, then, does Porter's approach assist in our understanding of the Far Eastern economies? He is interested in measuring national economic success by the existence of industries which possess a significant share of their respective export markets, and the export-orientated industrialisation of many East Asian countries do provide good test cases of his principal ideas. In this volume, Dong-Sung Cho reassesses the theoretical framework to be found in *The Competitive Advantage of Nations*, most notably the 'diamond', and he extends Porter's analysis of South Korea. Yoshitaka Suzuki investigates the nature of Porter's evidence, and questions whether Japan's competitive advantage has depended upon the emergence of industrial clusters manufacturing high value, differentiated products. Chia Siow Yue analyses Singapore's economy in 'Porterean' terms, and reviews the impact of government intervention and the influence of clustering. Gordon Redding argues that the example of Hong Kong, its mainly family-run businesses and Confucian culture fit uneasily within the schema presented by Porter. Lawrence Lau uses aggregate national statistics and measures of productivity to confirm the usefulness of competitive advantage as a concept, and he emphasises the way in which an absence of natural resources has beneficially induced Taiwan to depend instead on created endowments, human capital, and structural flexibility. The interpretative and evidential value of *The Competitive Advantage of Nations* is accepted, but the contributors are not without criticism. They seek to build upon Porter's impressive edifice and to broaden the interpretations and approaches of the debate. As a consequence, they pose questions on the specific patterns and pathways of newly industrialising economies; on the creation of factor conditions, human capital and core infrastructure; and on the role of national culture, models of organisational sociology, and the necessary functions of the state.

Firstly, all of Porter's three major works lucidly discuss choices of corporate strategy, and the creation of competitive advantage and its contribution to success at the level of the company is convincingly explored. *The Competitive Advantage of Nations* is Porter's most interesting and important work, because he is attempting to explain the comparative success of whole economies and the concomitant rise of globally competitive industries in particular countries. Within the 'diamond', companies and industrial clusters – displayed along the vertical axis – interact with those supply-side and demand-side macro-economic factors – on the horizontal axis – that mould the business environment (see Figure 1). This interaction encourages the growth of specific industries with the capacity to underpin national economies, whilst other sectors are discouraged by the prevailing macroeconomic environment, and Porter is better at exploring the origins of company-based capabilities than the roots of factor and demand conditions. Within emerging nations, the seeming inability of companies and markets to achieve widespread and balanced industrial transformation, if left to themselves, is central to debates in development economics. The barriers of disadvantageous national circumstances and rivalry from overseas multinationals prevent the emergence of indigenous companies and industries with globally competitive organisational capabilities in management skills, research and development, technology, and finance. Industrial development is at best patchy, reliant on cheap labour, or marked by income disparity; it is not reminiscent of the modern economic growth which Kuznets defines. A more detailed historical investigation of individual countries and their economic progress is required, and Porter admits that his book falls short of the standards demanded of a professional historian,[15] though, to be fair, he has been a leading exponent of the corporate case-study method. A strength of Chandler's *Scale and Scope* is its description of how large-scale businesses grew alongside changes in national economies. The adoption of mass production strategies and multidivisional organisational structures by certain companies were a direct response to specific, delineated developments in supply and demand factors, initially in the United States, then Britain and Germany.[16]

By emphasising the vertical axis of the 'diamond', Porter seems to be leaving many elements along his horizontal plane as a number of 'givens' (see Cho, Suzuki and Redding in this volume). Although his analysis of factor-, investment- and innovation-driven stages in competitive development does provide some insight into their origins, Porter's framework and evidence can be more aptly applied to advanced industrial nations, where competitive rivalry, technological up-grading and clustering within an already established, complex economic infrastructure and sophisticated and high levels of consumer demand may be the leading issues. In the Japan of the inter-war period and in the immediate post-war years, and within the developing economies of the Far East, company rivalry and market mechanisms may only partially explain economic development, and certainly not the speed with which development was achieved. Attention must be paid to market 'substitutes' such as government agency, protective measures and cooperative, even collusive arrangements, as well as the activities of individual private enterprise, and these may account for many critical developmental gains in educational standards, the channelling of capital, technology acquisition, and research and development. Dong-Sung Cho has adopted Porter's 'diamond' to take account of the Korean experience. Given that country's lack of natural resources and its small domestic market, he argues that human, supply-side factors were the mainspring of economic success. The role of workers and labour productivity, politicians and state bureaucrats, entrepreneurial business leaders, and professional managers and engineers, each in its turn, created the ability to establish Porter's infrastructure, demand conditions, corporate capabilities, and clusters. Cho offers his nine-factor model in place of the four major factors located on the 'diamond', arguing that for the Far East and many developing nations it has greater explanatory power. Many of the same points are made by Chia Siow Yue in her description of Singapore's competitive advantages and their evolution. Furthermore, although Japan's massive domestic market has directly assisted the development of organisational capabilities, the long-term contribution of demand conditions in Korea and Taiwan is not yet evident. But the island economies of Singapore and Hong Kong possess small markets and require open trading relationships, and this fact contradicts to some extent the emphasis placed on domestic demand conditions within Porter's diamond.

It follows, secondly, that Porter may be underestimating the particular contribution made by national governments to the East Asian 'miracle'. None of the chapters in this volume describe a story of state-directed development, but the Far Eastern state is seen at particular junctures as significant to the establishment of private enterprise and globally competitive industries. The literature on Japan's Ministry of Finance and the Ministry of International Trade and Industry continues to grow, as does the historical debate on their importance relative to the activities of highly competitive corporations. But close business–government relations have enabled the formation of industrial strategies and cooperative ventures in steel, shipbuilding, and oil, and current projects include VLSI circuits and biotechnology. The Japanese state has evinced a pragmatic, institutional and company-level approach to economic policy, and government assistance, the *keiretsu* structures, and joint ventures have been used as practical and necessary market 'substitutes', especially in the early development of industrial capability.[17] Now that Japan falls within the category of advanced nation, MITI can be viewed, rightly or wrongly, as in the throes of an 'identity crisis'.[18] Governmental intervention, argues Chia, has been an unquestionable catalyst of Singapore's transformation: it has not only provided a non-corrupt, regulatory framework and an envied social consensus, but it has led initiatives in industrial relations, telecommunications, and transport infrastructure, in addition to those in labour training, managerial and technical education, research and development, investment, and the targeting of support for industrial clusters. Since the early 1960s, the Korean government has attempted to manage its economy like a military campaign, and, in the search for economic growth, it has successively challenged and conceded its reliance on the *chaebol*.[19] Cho emphasises the role of politicians and state bureaucrats, and illustrates their involvement in the semiconductor, automobile, steel and apparel industries. In the history and nature of government–business relationships, there are parallels with early stages of development in Taiwan, though there are obvious differences in the scale of state intervention and in the size and structure of Taiwanese industry.[20] Lau believes that flexible market mechanisms and an export-orientation have given its small, family-owned firms a sustained competitive advantage, and the role of government is by necessity more restrained. Nonetheless, in the absence of large-scale firms possessing substantial resources, the state has coordinated and will increasingly have to encourage research and development if the Taiwanese economy is to progress. Amongst Japan and the Four Tigers, the non-interventionist regime of Hong Kong is, as Redding points out, the exception and not the norm. It is palliative to note how the two island nations and ethnically Chinese entrepots of Singapore and Hong Kong have followed different pathways in political economy with mutually successful results; a comparison that reveals the possibilities of developmental 'substitutes'.

Thirdly, while Porter mentions the influence of national cultures on economic success, Redding argues that he underplays and misinterprets its import. He states that business objectives and organisation are altered and shaped by prevailing cultural attributes, and that it is both sociologically necessary and economically rational that they utilise or become embedded in national views on authority, trust and identity. Porter is attempting to provide a universal theoretical framework, but Redding and others interpret his viewpoint as ethnocentric and Anglo-American. Expanding on the perspectives of organisational sociology, Redding describes how the Chinese family enterprise, its structures and operations may be founded in a particular culture. As a result, he challenges Porter's very units of analysis: the networked nature of Chinese business activities make it difficult to isolate individual firms, and, as Hong Kong is such an open economy and because it is so closely integrated with southern China, it is impossible to speak of its *national* competitive advantages. Hong Kong presents a methodological problem which, perhaps, only the arrival of 1997 and its secession to China can resolve.[21] Redding believes that the relationship between cultural attributes, business organisation and economic success has produced many varieties of capitalism. His perspective is potentially oppositional to the discovery of those differences in stages of economic growth, the need for market 'substitutes', business–state relations, and the contingent selections of pathways through which infrastructure and organisational capability can be created, as has been noted above. A sociological emphasis is distinguished from an economic one, despite influential attempts to unite both traditions.[22] Nevertheless, the points raised from the vantage point of development economics or national culture can both be usefully addressed by Porter.

Fourthly, Suzuki poses a further methodological issue to the ones raised by Redding. *The Competitive Advantage of Nations* is a study of seven countries, and its comparisons depend upon data collected in 1985. The book lacks a long-term, historical analysis, and Japan's obvious successes in the world markets of the mid-1980s may be a poor guide to its sustainable competitive advantages. Suzuki questions Porter's belief in the particularly 'systemic' management of the Japanese value-chain across many clusters, and the extent to which Japan, having reached the innovation-driven stage of economic development, has gained the more secure competitive advantages of product differentiation. He casts doubt on the depth and breadth of clustering which Porter attributes to this country, yet the emergence of supporting and related industries amongst national determinants of competitive advantage is critical to the gaining of the innovation stage and the manufacture of high-value products. Japan, says Suzuki, has depended and will continue to depend on price competitiveness, and any reliance on product differentiation was temporary to the mid-1980s and, outside a few sectors with relatively small aggregate sales, the cause of longer term disadvantage. He argues that the rise of the *yen* and the growing competitiveness of other East

Asian countries have undermined a number of Japanese industries. Chia, too, contends a lack of clustering in Singapore, and Porter has noted its failure to overcome competitive vulnerability through the establishment of indigenous industries.[23] Lau, in turn, wonders about the transitory characteristics of competitiveness in Taiwan, where sustained advantage in price-sensitive markets is the result of companies continuously entering new product areas. Suzuki's criticisms of his analysis of Japan – a test-case for Porter and his declared epitome of value-chain management, clustering and product differentiation – have greater implications.

Fifthly, Suzuki is concerned by the use of inexact terminology, most notably the definition of 'clusters', and the method by which Porter has selected 'globally-competitive industries' as evidence of national competitive advantage appears equally subjective. At the heart of this problem is one that often confronts practitioners of the social sciences. Porter is seeking to provide a universally applicable theory and framework, and there are strengths and benefits in concepts that are broad and enveloping, especially if the final objectives are comparative. Obvious weaknesses are the uncertainties of specific application, and, for analysts of the businesses and economies of the Far East and of developing countries, this is especially true of concepts which are sometimes seen as ethnocentric in their perspective. That said, this criticism and others made throughout this volume cannot detract from Porter's stature as the most influential living thinker on modern capitalism. Any ensuing debate on *The Competitive Advantage of Nations* is a tribute to a work which needs to be addressed, questioned and developed if the East Asian 'miracle' is to be fully understood.

NOTES

1. World Bank, *The East Asian Miracle: Economic Growth and Public Policy* (Oxford, 1993), pp.1–4.
2. S. Kuznets, *Modern Economic Growth: Rate, Structure and Spread* (Yale, 1966).
3. World Bank, *East Asian Miracle*, passim.
4. See, for example, A. Gershenkron, *Economic Backwardness in Historical Perspective: A Book of Essays* (Cambridge, Mass., 1966).
5. C. Johnson, *MITI and the Japanese Miracle* (Stanford, 1982); A.H. Amsden, *Asia's Next Giant: South Korea and Late Industrialisation* (New York, 1989); R. Wade, *Governing the Market: Economic Theory and the Role of Government in East Asian Industrialisation* (Princeton, 1990); T.B. Gold, *State and Society in the Taiwan Miracle* (New York, 1986).
6. P. Arestis and M. Sawyer (eds.), *A Biographical Dictionary of Dissenting Economists* (Aldershot, 1992); R.E. Lane, *The Market Experience* (Cambridge, 1991).
7. World Bank, *East Asian Miracle*, pp.157–257, 352–4.
8. M.E. Porter, *Competitive Strategy: Techniques for Analyzing Industries and Competitors* (Cambridge, Mass., 1980).
9. M.E. Porter, *Competitive Advantage: Creating and Sustaining Superior Performance* (New York, 1985).
10. A.D. Chandler, *Strategy and Structure: Chapters in the History of Industrial Enterprise* (Cambridge, Mass., 1962); *The Visible Hand: The Managerial Revolution in American*

Business (Cambridge, Mass., 1977); and *Scale and Scope: The Dynamics of Industrial Capitalism* (Cambridge, Mass., 1990).
11. M.E. Porter, *The Competitive Advantage of Nations* (London, 1990).
12. Nonetheless, a debate on modern organisational forms can be found in C.A. Bartlett, 'Building and Managing the Transnational: The New Organisational Challenge' in M.E. Porter (ed.), *Competition in Global Industries* (Boston, 1986), pp.367–401.
13. Porter, *Competitive Advantage of Nations*, esp. pp.69–130.
14. Ibid., pp.543–73.
15. Ibid, p.28.
16. Chandler, *Scale and Scope*, passim.
17. Johnson, *MITI*, and 'Comparative Capitalism: The Japanese Difference', *California Management Review* (Summer, 1993), pp.51–67; G.G. Hamilton and M. Orru, 'Organisational Structures of East Asian Companies' in K.H. Chung and H.K. Lee (eds.), *Korean Managerial Dynamics* (New York, 1989); T. Kikkawa, 'Kigyo Shudan: the Formation and Functions of Enterprise Groups' in E. Abe and R. Fitzgerald (eds.), *The Birth of the Japanese Management System* (forthcoming); P. O'Brien, 'Industry Structure as a Competitive Advantage: the History of Japan's Post-war Steel Industry' in C. Harvey and G. Jones (eds.), *Organisational Capability and Competitive Advantage* (London, 1992), pp.128–59; H. Morikawa, *Zaibatsu* (Tokyo, 1992); Y. Suzuki, *Japanese Management Structures, 1920–80* (London, 1991); P.A. Genther, *A History of Japan's Business-Government Relationship: The Passenger Car Industry* (Michigan, 1990); M. Anchordoguy, *Computers Inc.: Japan's Challenge to IBM* (Cambridge, Mass., 1989); M. Fransman, *The Market and Beyond: Cooperation and Competition in Information Technology in the Japanese System* (Cambridge, 1990).
18. See, for example, *The Economist*, 22 Jan. 1994, pp.61–2.
19. Amsden, *Asia's Next Giant* K.H. Jung, 'Business-Government Relations in Korea' in K.H. Chung and H.C. Lee (eds.), *Korean Managerial Dynamics* (New York, 1989), pp.11–26; L.P. Jones and I. Sakong, *Government, Business and Entrepreneurship in Economic Development: The Korea Case* (Boston, 1980).
20. Y.C. Jao, V. Mok and L.S. Ho (eds.), *Economic Development in Chinese Societies: Models and Experiences* (Hong Kong, 1989); W.Galenson (ed.), *Economic Growth and Structural Change in Taiwan: the Postwar Experiences of the Republic of China* (Ithaca, 1979); L.J. Lau, *Models of Development: A Comparative Study of Economic Growth in South Korea and Taiwan* (San Francisco, 1990).
21. S.G. Redding, *The Spirit of Chinese Capitalism* (New York, 1990); R.D. Whitley, *Business Systems in East Asia: Firms, Markets and Societies* (London, 1992).
22. M. Grannovetter, 'Economic Action and Social Structure: The Problem of Embeddedness', *American Journal of Sociology* (1985), Vol.91, pp.481–510.
23. Porter, *Competitive Advantage of Nations*, p.566.

A Dynamic Approach to International Competitiveness: The Case of Korea

DONG-SUNG CHO

INTRODUCTION

Michael Porter's recent work helps explain the sources of international competitiveness possessed by the economies of advanced nations, but has a limited application when it comes to explaining the levels and dynamic changes of economies in less developed or developing countries. The experience of Korea's economic development in the past three decades reveals how groups of well-educated, motivated, and dedicated people have played a central role in not only shaping the nation's competitiveness but also moving the nation dynamically from a less developed stage to an advanced one. If we modify Porter's diamond model to take account of the Korean experience, we are left with a new paradigm of international competitiveness. It divides sources of international competitiveness into two broad categories: 'physical' factors and 'human' factors. By 'physical' factors, we refer to endowed resources, the business environment, related and supporting industries, and domestic demand, which together determine the level of international competitiveness of a given nation at a given time. Human factors include workers, politicians and bureaucrats, entrepreneurs, and professional managers and engineers. By creating, motivating and controlling the four physical elements, these human factors drive the national economy from one stage of international competitiveness to the next. An external factor of pure chance is added to these eight internal factors to make the new paradigm a nine-factor model. As we shall see, this new framework can elucidate the sources of economic growth in less developed countries as well as those dynamic changes in international competitiveness that are associated with economic growth. The relative importance of each of the eight physical and human factors changes as the national economy moves from a less developed stage to a developing stage, to a semi-developed stage, and, finally, to a fully developed stage.

When a nation's trade balance swings from surplus to deficit, its people begin to worry about an economic decline and associate it with a diminution in the nation's international competitiveness. Governments can point to uncontrollable, or external factors such as a slowdown in the international economy or high exchange rates as the cause of trade deficits

---

Dong-Sung Cho, Seoul National University

and weakened international competitiveness. Businessmen would take advantage of this occasion to demand tax cuts and the imposition of import barriers as corrective measures. However, trade balance and international competitiveness are not the same. There are nations which suffer from weak international competitiveness, whilst possessing balanced trade accounts or even, as a result of import controls, trade surpluses. Some nations have demonstrable international competitiveness, but reveal occasional trade deficits. Lastly, international competitiveness is not determined by external factors alone. Under the same global economic environment, some nations gain market share at the expense of others. In this paper the term 'international competitiveness' is defined in a way that systematically explains the long-term resilience of a nation's economy. Next, a new paradigm is formulated, and it is composed of the nine factors which determine the international competitiveness of a nation as it moves from a less developed stage to a developing stage, to a semi-developed stage, and finally to a developed stage. Then, the model is applied to Korea and to the development of its four major industries at different stages of international competitiveness. The final part of this paper looks at policies to improve international competitiveness.

THE THEORETICAL BACKGROUND TO INTERNATIONAL COMPETITIVENESS

A Definition of International Competitiveness

One misconception of international competitiveness is based on the notion that it depends on a plentiful supply of labour, capital and natural resources at low prices.[1] This economic theory mistakenly links a nation's international competitiveness to its factor endowments. Endowed resources are only a part of many determinant factors. There are countries with plentiful resources but a weak economy. In a world in which raw materials, capital and even labour move across national borders, the possession of endowed resources alone does not determine international competitiveness. Another misconception is to measure a nation's international competitiveness by its share of world markets.[2] While a useful indicator, it is often misleading because a nation's share of world markets can rise regardless of its international competitiveness. A nation may arbitrarily raise its market share by lowering export prices below production costs, sometimes through government subsidies, but its international competitiveness is not necessarily strengthened. As we have seen, trade balances have limited value in this debate.[3] Some nations register large if temporary trade deficits, despite their maintaining competitiveness when they are confronted with political or international difficulties. A good illustration is the Federal Republic of Germany in the early 1990s which had to carry trade deficits while undergoing unification with East Germany. On the other hand, Middle East nations showed extravagant trade surpluses during the energy crises of the 1970s, but their industries generally lacked international competitiveness. Trading accounts are inappropriate indicators, at least in the short term, of industrial strength. One widespread misconception is to divide international competitiveness into two categories: price competitiveness, such as nominal wages, exchange rates and labour productivity; and non-price competitiveness, such as quality, marketing, service and market differentiation.[4] In order to gauge price competitiveness, export price, production cost, and consumer or wholesale price indices are used. Rising prices are seen as weakening a nation's international competitiveness. In reality there are cases in which nations with strong international competitiveness can and do raise the price of their products. Quality status, durability, design and consumer satisfaction are used to evaluate non-price competitiveness, but there are no empirical studies to prove their influence. Price and non-price factors are not the causes but the results of a nation's international competitiveness.

In summary, traditional views cover only a part of many factors determining the level of international competitiveness, or mistake results for causes.[5] A new definition of international competitiveness is required and it should include all of the major factors in a holistic, systematic manner if the causal relations between the factors and the resulting level of a nation's competitiveness are to be discovered. The international competitiveness of a national industry can be defined by its having a superior market position through high profits and constant growth when compared to competitors. A country cannot possess international competitiveness simply because it has one or two successful industries. Sri Lanka has a well-developed trade in tea growing and processing, and Iceland is the centre of a strong fish processing industry, yet few would argue that these two nations have international competitiveness. A nation needs to have a multitude of industries with strong competitiveness. Nor can a nation be regarded as internationally competitive if her industries are strong because of some external factors. The United States, in the 1945–70 period, enjoyed an uncontested position in most of the industries which were reliant upon high levels of technology and vast domestic markets. A nation needs the sources of competitiveness which can be applied to a number of industries. A nation, then, is internationally competitive when it has many industries with competitive advantage based on common domestic sources of competitiveness.

Existing Studies on Determinants of International Competitiveness

Studies on determinants of international competitiveness are mostly predicated on theories of international trade which focus on the comparative cost of production, natural resources, and technologies.[6] Since each nation has different comparative advantages, scholars have not succeeded in finding a general theory that can explain the economic fortune of countries with a small number of generic, universally applicable factors. In the early 1960s, economists began to recognise how a nation's international competitiveness could be affected not only by its trade, but also by overseas direct investment undertaken by multinational enterprises. Theories of foreign direct investment subsequently proliferated. Concepts of monopolistic advantages have identified ownership-specific advantages such as technology, marketing know-how, management skills, financial resources, and scale economies as the sources of competitiveness uniquely possessed by multinationals.[7] On the other hand, industrial organisation theory has demonstrated market imperfections or failures to be the main spur of foreign direct investment and the origins of the advantages exercised by multinational enterprises.[8] By concentrating on a particular type of business organisation both approaches failed to explain the sources of national competitive advantage in a comprehensive and systematic manner. Dunning integrated these independently evolved theories in order to explain comprehensively all the advantages possessed of multinational enterprises. He outlined the changing investment patterns which a nation may undergo as it moves from one stage of development to the next. But he does not deal with the importance of international competitiveness in relation to stages of national development.[9] Buckley and Casson have discussed the evolving role of specific factors which determine the success of multinational enterprises operating in foreign markets, but their discussion is limited to issues of geography and entrepreneurial culture.[10] In answer to these shortcomings new more systematic studies on international competitiveness have been produced by Kogut, Goldsmith and Clutterbuck, and Yamazawa. They have presented the determinants of international competitiveness at the level of individual companies, but they do not show how these develop into the macro-level advantages of a nation or industry.[11]

The link was first demonstrated by Porter. He pointed out that classical trade theories based on comparative advantage did not satisfactorily explain the trade patterns of resource-poor countries like Japan. Then he presented his model of international competitiveness, based on the 'diamond'.[12] The model is composed of four determinants: factor conditions; firm strategy, structure, and rivalry; related and supporting industries; and demand conditions. Besides these four, Porter cites chance and government as additional factors. In essence, this model shows how an industry can maintain international competitiveness when these determinants are in place, but it must be said that Porter's theory primarily explains the economies of advanced nations. His model needs to be modified for it to be applied to developing or less developed nations, because the countries have to create international competitiveness without necessarily having any of the four determinants in place. Porter's analysis cannot explain the success which Korea and Taiwan have achieved in the second half of the twentieth century. A new model will serve two objectives: one is better to evaluate which elements have contributed to the international competitiveness of less developed economies; the other is to show how a nation can improve its national advantage.

A NEW MODEL OF INTERNATIONAL COMPETITIVENESS FOR LESS DEVELOPED COUNTRIES

The Nine-Factor Model

In order to assess Korea's international competitiveness, two major considerations should be addressed. Government and businesses had to introduce capital and technology from foreign countries or create resources and other factors influencing economic growth from their initial stages. The key engine of Korea's economic growth has been an abundant and diverse group of people with generally high levels of education, motivation and dedication to work. Korea's population can be grouped into four: workers; politicians and bureaucrats who formulate and implement economic plans; enterpreneurs who make investment decisions despite

FIGURE 1

A NEW PARADIGM OF INTERNATIONAL COMPETITIVENESS
(THE NINE FACTOR MODEL)

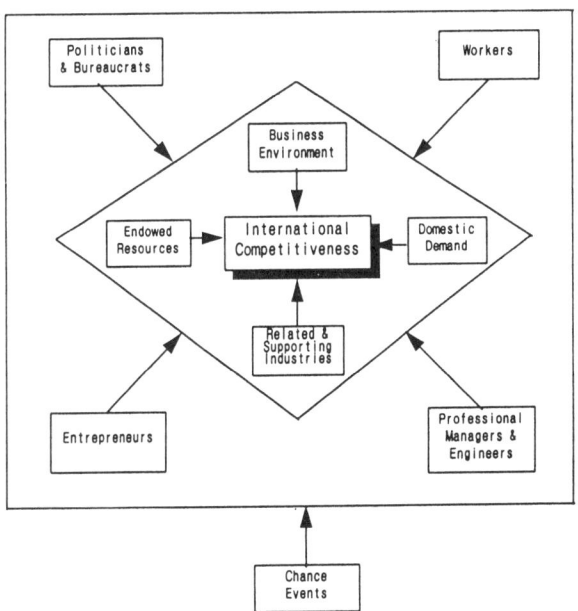

high risks; and professional managers who are in charge of operations and engineers who implement new technologies. To appreciate their contribution to Korea's development, a nine-factor model is required. There are four physical determinants of international competitiveness, namely endowed resources, the business environment, related and supporting industries and domestic demand; there are also four human factors namely workers, politicians and bureaucrats, entrepreneurs and professional managers and engineers. External chance events should be noted as the ninth factor (see Figure 1).

The difference between the new model and Porter's diamond model is to be found as much in the division of factors as in the addition of new ones. The diamond included both natural resources and labour in factor conditions, but the nine factor model places natural resources under endowed resources, while labour is included within the category of workers. A detailed investigation of the nine factors of international competitiveness is needed.

FIGURE 2

COMPARISON OF THE DIAMOND AND THE NINE FACTOR MODEL

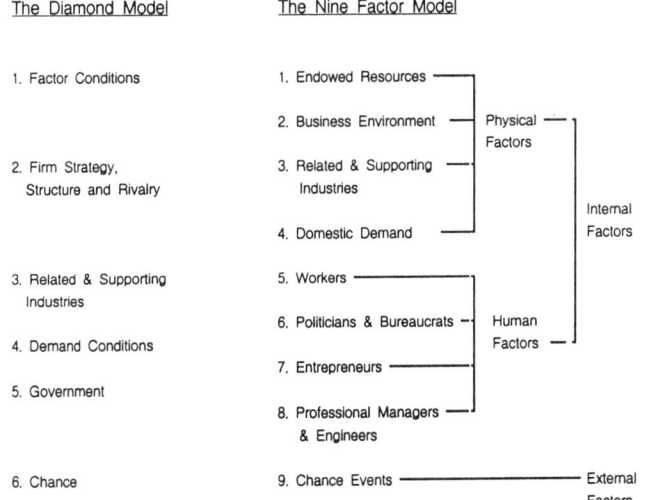

(i) Physical Factors

(a) *Endowed resources* can be divided into mineral, agricultural, forestry, fishery and environmental resources. Mineral resources are depletable, and energy resources such as coal, oil and natural gas can be distinguished from non-energy resources such as iron ore, gold and silver. Agriculture, forests and fish stocks are renewable and environmental factors are composed of land, weather, water and other natural advantages.[13] All these resources can form inputs into economic activities, and they may add to a nation's international competitiveness.

(b) *Business environment*. The business environment should be viewed at the levels of nation, industry and company. At the national level, there are visible and invisible components: the first includes roads, ports, telecommunications and other forms of infrastructure; the second is concerned with the people's acceptance of competitive values and market mechanisms and the commitment of producers, merchants, consumers and other participants in the economy to the legitimacy and obligations of commercial deals and credit. At an industrial level, the business environment is determined by the number and size of competitors, the type and height of entry barriers, the degree of product differentiation, and other factors shaping the nature of rivalry and economic activity. At a company level, the strategy and organisation of businesses and the attitudes and behaviour of individuals and groups within enterprises are major considerations.[14]

(c) *Related and supporting industries*. Related industries can be divided into vertically related industries and horizontally related industries. While one ecompasses the influence of upstream and downstream stages of production, the other is concerned with industries that use the same technology, raw materials, distribution networks or marketing activities. Supporting industries include financial, insurance, information, transportation and other service sectors.[15]

(d) *Domestic demand* includes both quantitative and qualitative aspects. The size of domestic market determines minimum economies of scale for indigenous companies, as well as the stability of demand. The home economy acts as a test market for products that can be shipped overseas, and the risks of international commerce are reduced. Greater benefits can be gained from the qualitative dimensions. The expectations of consumers can stimulate competitiveness, and, in a nation where consumers have sophisticated and strict standards on product quality in addition to a high degree of consumerism, its businesses can accrue international advantages in the course of satisfying demanding home conditions.[16]

(ii) Human Factors

It is the human factors which mobilise the above-mentioned physical factors. People combine and arrange the physical factors with the aim of obtaining international competitiveness. Workers, politicians and bureaucrats, entrepreneurs, and professional managers and engineers have to be considered.

(a) *Workers*. The most easily identified measure of the worth of workers is the wage level, yet it is only one of the many attributes which directly or indirectly affect labour productivity. Others are levels of education, a sense of belonging to an organisation, acceptance of authority, a work ethic, and the size of the labour pool. The traditional explanation of Korea's comparative advantage in cheap labour from the 1960s to the mid-1980s overlooked more fundamental factors such as high education levels, discipline and the work ethic.

(b) *Politicians and bureaucrats*. Politicians seek to win and maintan power, and economic development is one of the many routes they can choose for achieving their primary objective. Nations governed by politicians that are committed to growth and success can assist in the creation of international competitiveness. China in the late 1980s and 1990s is a manifestation of how a national economy can benefit from leaders that appreciate the value of economic development, even under a Communistic system. In general, an efficient and non-corrupt bureaucracy can assist the application of state policy, and can make a substantial addition to international competitiveness.

(c) *Entrepreneurs*. As entrepreneurs venture on new businesses despite a high degree of risk, they are distinct from ordinary businessmen. They are essential to any nation at an early stage of economic development. Over time, a country's competitiveness is strengthened by their efforts to diminish risks and maximise returns.

(d) *Professional managers and engineers*. When international competition necessitates fierce price cutting and a search for enhanced service, risk-taking attitude alone will not bring deeply entrenched competitiveness. The dedicated work of professional managers in reducing production costs by even small fractions and the cutting of delivery times determines the future of nations as well as individual businesses.

(iii) The External Factor: Chance Events

Chance events are unpredictable changes in the environment, often unassociated with the international business system. They include unexpected breakthroughs in new technologies or products, oil shocks, sharp fluctuations in world capital markets or foreign exchange rates, changes in the policies of foreign governments, movements in international demands, and the outbreak of war. Physical and human factors have in many cases to be reconfigured if a nation is to maintain competitiveness, or take the opportunity to improve competitive advantage.

The Life Cycle of National Competitiveness

We can evaluate a nation's international competitiveness by judging the influence which the nine factors may have, and we can similarly begin to understand its development. A nation's economic status is determined by its international competitiveness and the nine factors have varying weights as a country moves from a less-developed stage to a developing stage, then to a semi-developed stage, and finally to a developed stage.[17] A model framework of the life cycle of national competitiveness is shown in Figure 3, and a review of the characteristics prevalent in each stage and the major sources of competitive advantage at each juncture will be valuable.

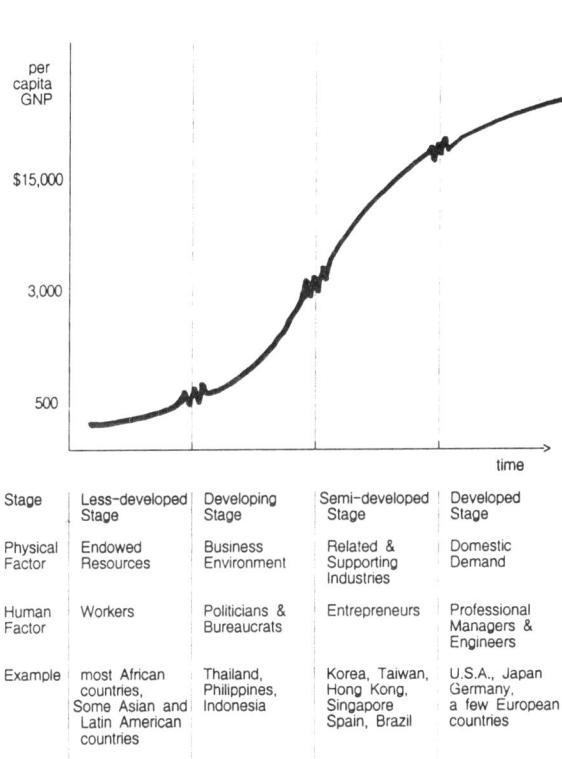

FIGURE 3
LIFE CYCLE OF NATIONAL COMPETITIVENESS

(i) Less Developed Stage

Countries prior to economic development have only limited endowed and labour resources, and they tend to lack the management know-how and technology which can put these assets into production processes that can generate value-added. It follows that they lack international competitiveness, and nations with a per capita income of less than US$500 in 1990 are to be found in this category, a number of African and Southwest Asian nations being exemplary. Although most of the Central and South American nations have per capita incomes of more than $500, a few do belong to this group. These nations cannot implement stable economic policies because of frequent changes of power and other political uncertainties, although they do possess considerable natural resources and quite sizeable labour pools.

(ii) Developing Stage

The developing stage, when a nation is at the early period of development, sees the inertia of a less developed economy being overcome by politicians beginning to fulfil political ambition through policies of growth and construction. In the process, they mobilise bureaucrats to carry out industrial policies, and enhance the business environment through the creation of financial markets and social infrastructures. Sometimes, endowed resources and available workforces are channelled into government-run enterprises, and a nation has its first opportunity to strengthen international competitiveness. Businesses tend to introduce production technology from foreign countries and they also depend on foreign markets for the sale of products. As a result, a nation's international competitiveness in this stage largely rests on changes in the international business environment, including foreign exchange rates and the prices of raw materials. Because businesses are still establishing organisational capacity and facing strong competition in world markets, the government frequently allocates scarce resources to one or two companies in each industry. Most industries at this stage of development are monopolised by a single or a few enterprises.

The process of founding international competitiveness through collaboration between politicians and bureaucrats can be seen in the case of Korea during the 1960s. President Park Chung-Hee, who assumed power as a result of a military coup, had to cope with the abrupt suspension of economic assistance from the United States, which disapproved of his military regime. Park believed that to keep power he had to reduce huge trade deficits. He formulated and implemented a series of Five-Year Economic Development Plans from 1962 onwards, designed to invest resources in selected strategic industries, and, in order to improve the business environment, highways, ports, subways and other essential social infrastructure were built. Companies were encouraged to develop manufacturing facilities in textiles, footwear, steel, electronics, machinery and automobiles, and received financial support and payment guarantees from the government. Nations at the developing stage show a per capita income of between US$500 and US$3,000, and include Korea and Taiwan in the 1960s through to the early 1970s, and Thailand, Malaysia, Indonesia, and the Philippines in the 1990s.

(iii) Semi-Developed Stage

As economic development passes the early period, a capitalist system may allow entrepreneurs to make bold investments despite associated high risks, and they begin to reduce their dependence on the government. In other words, monopoly rents do not accrue only to state-supported enterprises, and the business environment has become favourable to the process of active investment. Entrepreneurs are prepared to invest and seek to achieve economies of scale. If necessary, they borrow resources from overseas. While nations with abundant natural resources will take advantage of them, those at a semi-developed stage may secure essential in-puts at low prices through long-term contracts or direct resource development. As a result of these efforts, the latter's international competitiveness can become stronger than that of the former. The human factors which form the main source of international competitiveness include risk-taking entrepreneurs. An oligopolistic pattern of competition appears amongst businesses at the semi-developed stage, and companies tend to diversify into new areas from their initial, successful base, resulting in the further development of related and supporting industries. The international competitiveness of industries is enhanced by the strengthening of these linkages. Nations at this stage have a per capita income in the range of US$3,000 to US$15,000, and are evidenced by Japan in the 1960s and the so-called newly industrialising economies of Korea, Taiwan, Hong Kong and Singapore in the 1990s.

(iv) Developed Stage

Following the innovation of manufacturing processes, products and business organisations in the semi-developed stage, the connections among horizontally and vertically related and supporting industries are further enhanced. The goods and services of these industries can enter competitive international markets on equal terms with those from advanced countries. Manufacturing processes become more sophisticated, product quality is improved and a balanced development between upstream and downstream areas is achieved. The role of entrepreneurs becomes less important, as professional managers and engineers develop their businesses and increase efficiency. Sectors that are horizontally and vertically related to initially successful industries become internationally competitive, and government controls such as the artificial allocation of funds, market protection and the payment of subsidies, are gradually phased out. The wage pressures from workers do intensify, as does competition from innovations in marketing, product quality and sales service. As income levels rise, consumers make more demands for better quality and services. Per capita incomes of more than US$15,000 are apparent in developed nations, which comprise the United States, Japan, Germany and other West European countries.

The Life Cycle of Industrial Competitiveness

As can be seen from the above analysis, international competitiveness is determined by four physical factors – endowed resources, the business environment, related and supporting industries and domestic demand and these are created, mobilised and controlled by the four human factors – workers, politicians and bureaucrats, entrepreneurs, and professional managers and engineers. These eight factors play different roles in the different stages of a nation's economic development. Each nation's economy also consists of primary, secondary and tertiary sectors, and the balance of activity between them differs between different stages of development. The stage and speed of each industry's development differs according to the nation's overall business environment. In order to appreciate each nation's international competitiveness more fully an analysis of industries is needed to supplement the macro-perspective. An industry's international competitiveness is strengthened or weakened according to changes in the business environment and the specific responses of human actors. A static approach using the nine factors requires a dynamic analysis based on the life cycle of industrial competitiveness. Industries move from an early stage to a growth stage, to a maturing stage, and finally to a declining stage[18] The physical and human factors of international competitiveness have varying influences as each industry passes through different phases.

(i) Early Stage

In general, an industry is at an early stage if its sources of competition are limited to endowed resources, such as abundant mineral resources, and ample and fertile land. Despite their availability, some countries cannot utilise their given attributes due to insufficient know-how and technology. An industry gains growth potential by making lower priced products and using unprocessed resources and labour.

(ii) Growth Stage

To transfer from the early stage to a growth stage, industries need politicians and bureaucrats who are willing to support businesses systematically. Politicans and bureaucrats create a business environment favourable to active investment, select certain industries for advancement, provide administrative and financial support, tax credits, insurance and information services and payment guarantees to chosen entrepreneurs. They sometimes protect particular industries until enough demand becomes captive or until access to foreign technology has been won. The market is organised on monopolistic or oligopolistic lines.

INTERNATIONAL COMPETITIVENESS OF KOREA 29

(iii) Maturing Stage

Innovation occurs in manufacturing processes, product development, and business organisation. Connections among horizontally and vertically related industries become stronger at this stage, and businesses which pursue a balanced development in both downstream and upstream areas remain competitive in international markets. Entrepreneurs take a leading role in a system reliant on active investment. This stage comes at a time when an industry's international competitiveness is extended to horizontally and vertically related industries, and government measures, such as the artificial allocation of investment capital, market protection and the payment of subsidies, are phased out. Industries embrace full competition from both domestic and foreign firms and the ensuing competition stimulates product development and quality improvements.

(iv) Declining Stage

An industry that passes through the maturing stage and fails to maintain innovation naturally enters a declining stage. Markets are saturated at this point and consumers' expectations for product quality are high. Production costs rise if businesses try to meet sophisticated consumer demands, resulting in a fast decline in their international competitiveness. Industries can correct these problems if professional managers and engineers cooperate to achieve organisational and technological innovations.[19]

CASE STUDIES: KOREA'S MAJOR INDUSTRIES

Figure 4 illustrates the above-mentioned life cycle of industrial competitiveness as applied to Korean industries which have had, presently possess, or are expected to achieve international competitiveness. The four cases studied were made to represent each stage of the industry life cycle: semiconductors belong to the early stage; automobiles to the growth stage, steel to a maturing stage, and apparel to a declining stage.

The Semiconductor Industry

Korea's semiconductor industry began in 1965 with the establishment of a joint venture called Komy Semiconductor. The string of factories established by US or Japanese firms to assemble simple transistors performed simple assembly processes requiring little technological input.[20] The only source of international competitiveness at this early phase was various labour attributes such as low wages, work discipline, and an abundant supply of skilled manpower. Many workers had been previously employed and trained by companies in the apparel and home electronics industries, and they quickly adapted to semiconductors. Various tax incentive schemes and direct financial support from government attracted

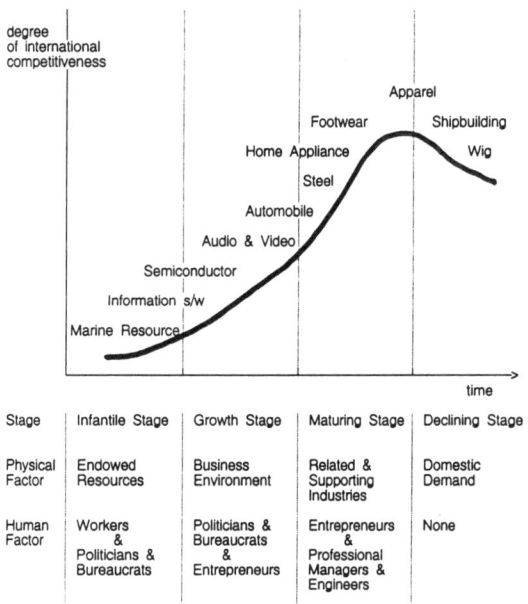

FIGURE 4
LIFE CYCLE OF INDUSTRIAL COMPETITIVENESS

foreign investment in this sector. In the growth period since 1978, Korea's semiconductor industry has been assisted by a variety of advantages: basic technologies were made available through joint ventures with foreign companies; Korean engineers, educated and trained in the United States and other advanced countries, returned; the government designated the industry to be strategically important, and provided companies with incentives for expansion and for research and development. Byung-Cheol Lee of the Samsung Group initiated a major investment in the industry at a time when nobody was sure of its success; and the spirit of rivalry amongst Samsung, Hyundai and Goldstar prompted additional developments in production and technology. The temporary shortage of electronic parts during the energy crisis of 1979 and the opportunities opened by the US–Japan Semiconductor Agreement in the US market benefited Korean semiconductor makers.

The Automobile Industry

Korea's automobile industry was founded in 1962 with a complete knock-down or kit mode of production with parts supplied by Honda and Toyota, and it reached a semi-knock-down stage in 1967. Soon, General Motors moved into Korea with a local assembly plant to tap the growing Korean market. Major sources of international competitiveness during this early stage were the skilled labour force, geographic proximity to the Japanese companies which Korean firms were emulating, and industrial policies banning the importation of assembled cars and providing indigenous exporters with tax incentives. In essence, Korea's automobile industry gained its growth potential through the correct combination of foreign capital and technologies, joint international ventures, and government industrial policy. In 1975, a new company entered the industry. It was the Hyundai Motor Company which chose a strategy very different to the existing manufacturers. Instead of depending on the foreign capital and technology being offered through a joint venture proposed by Ford, Chairman Ju-Young Chung of the Hyundai Group decided that the company should construct its own plant with the money earned from construction and shipbuilding. It was a bold attempt with high risks, but in return it provided the company with the invaluable asset of independence and autonomy at a point when it was beginning to penetrate overseas markets. Unlike Mazda and Ford-affiliated Kia or GM-affiliated Daewoo, Hyundai could move into and export to any part of the world. In the 1980s, Hyundai made an inroad into the American and European markets and firmly established itself as one of the major automobile makers of the world.

Major sources of competitive advantage in the growth stage since the mid-1970s came from Chung's aggressive investment in production facilities and overseas marketing, the integration of subcontractors into the Hyundai family business and the development of indigenous technologies and original models. Although the government in 1980 disrupted the automobile industry by unsuccessfully mandating a merger between Hyundai and Daewoo and the closing of Kia, it later provided generous assistance in research and development and continued to protect the domestic market from an invasion of Japanese models. Other major factors underpinning expansion included the concurrent development of related industries such as steel, electric, electronic and machinery, as well as a growth in aggregate domestic demand.[21]

The Steel Industry

The history of Korea's steel industry has been the history of Pohang Iron and Steel Co. (POSCO). The industry's foundations are to be found before the First Five-Year Economic Development Plan in 1962, but it was not until the first phase of steel mill construction was completed in Ulsan in 1973 that the industry was firmly established. From that point, POSCO moved rapidly through the early stage. The industry was developed through an abundant labour force possessing skills and work discipline, foreign capital, the transfer of technologies from West European countries, and government assistance as exemplified most notably by the Steel Industry Promotion Law. The increase in steel demand was induced by the series of economic development plans, and the then President,

Park Chung-Hee, was convinced that the industry was fundamental to a number of related industries like automobiles, shipbuilding, electrics and electronics, and machinery. Chairman T.J. Park of POSCO was another important influence in his company's and industry's success.

The growth stage began after the second phase of construction at the Ulsan steel mill in 1978, when advanced steel-making countries were reducing their production capacities and modernising facilities. Major sources of international competitiveness during this stage were state industrial policies, the rise in domestic demand, and relative cost increases in US and Japanese firms. Most importantly, it was Chairman Park's leadership that drove POSCO's continued expansion, including the second steel plant at Kwangyang Bay, and he was determined to create a globally renowned company committed to product quality and managerial excellence. The maturing stage started in 1988 when major competitors in Japan, the US and Europe had completed their rationalisation programmes and concentrated on high value-added steel products. Korea sustained its international competitiveness in basic steel products, but its position in special steel categories was weakened. In response, POSCO increased efficiency and developed more expensive goods. Diversification strategies into telecommunications and other related and non-related industries were led by professional managers of POSCO in an attempt to broaden the company's commercial base.

The Apparel Industry

The apparel industry was one of Korea's earliest successful industries, and, in its early stage in the 1950s, major sources of competitiveness were found in a plentiful, cheap and dexterous labour force, post-war reconstruction projects by the government, state support for foreign loans and technology imports, and the knowledge already possessed in long-established firms. As the industry entered its growth stage in the 1960s, sources of advantage shifted to the high education levels of workers and their ability to adapt to new technologies, export-driven industrial policies, financial and tax benefits through the Textile Industry Promotion Law, investment and construction by entrepreneurs, and the growth in original engineering manufacture-based exports. Apparel makers transformed themselves into general trading companies such as Sunkyong, Hyosung, and Hanil,[22] and they assisted the penetration of foreign markets. A developing petrochemical industry then supplied high-quality artificial materials at competitive prices.

In the maturing stage of the 1980s, the United States enforced quotas on apparel imports, and the Korean government shifted priorities from light goods industries to heavy machinery, chemicals, and electronics. Wage levels increased in the course of Korea's rapid economic growth. The apparel industry had to face full and open competition, and mergers and acquisitions occurred. Independently or in partnership with general trading companies, manufacturers moved their plants to East Asian countries and the Caribbean islands, where production costs were lower and barriers to the US market could be avoided. Marketing subsidiaries were established overseas to facilitate and diversify export markets, and managerial policies have sustained the industry's competitiveness in the 1990s. Yet there are three areas of weakness: most sophisticated textile machines have to be imported; many closely related industries such as dyeing and fashion design are not internationally competitive; and, as a consequence, technologies and know-how in the manufacturing of top-quality apparel are lacking. Unless these deficiencies are remedied, the apparel industry will enter the declining stage.

CONCLUSION

A Comparison of Four Industries

If we compare the historical evolution of four industries, it is possible to identify the fact that major sources of competitiveness were identical at each stage of the industrial life cycle regardless of industry type. Major sources of advantage in the early stage of all four industries were the workers and politicians and bureaucrats. In the semiconductor industry, it was the labour content of production that persuaded foreign investors to establish a whole industry. In automobiles, it was the skilled workers and state industrial policies that attracted overseas interest and, in the steel industry, it was employee skills and disciplines and the commitment of the political leader. In apparel, an abundant supply of cheap and dexterous labour and the government's reconstruction objectives were determinant. The state remains a major source of competitiveness in the growth stage, but entrepreneurs become more influential than workers. In the semiconductor industry, the government designated it to be strategically important, providing incentives and subsidies for research and development, while the leadership of Chairman Lee of Samsung was critical. In automobiles, Japanese automobiles faced import barriers, and Chairman Chung established the Hyundai Motor as a major international producer. Government's policies and the management of Chairman Park turned POSCO into a global leader. In the apparel industry, the government provided financial assistance through an export promotion policy, while a number of entrepreneurs like Chairman Chey of Sunkyong created general trading companies.

As an industry moves to a maturing stage, the entrepreneurs continue to be crucial sources of strength, but government is less determinant than professional managers and engineers. The professional managers of POSCO slowly but steadily enhanced efficiency and diversified the business, while engineers led the development of high value-added products. In apparels, professional managers also brought about diversification in export markets, invested abroad, and penetrated local markets.

The Implications for the Korean Economy

The Korean economy possesses international competitiveness because it has a number of industries in the growth and maturing stages and common sources of advantage. In the life cycle of national competitiveness, it can be placed in the semi-developed stage category (see Figure 3), moving toward a developed stage. Nevertheless, Korea has been experiencing a major crisis in recent years, because the real wage level has more than doubled in just four years, the trade balance has evolved into a big deficit since 1989, and the rate of economic growth has slowed from a ten per cent level to less than six per cent in 1992. Koreans are very concerned about their economy deterioration before it reaches a par with advanced nations. What is the model telling us about Korea and its ability to reach a developed phase?

Workers and politicians and bureaucrats – the main forces of economic growth until now – should enable entrepreneurs and professional managers and engineers to take a lead. As the sources of economic growth moved from workers to government, and from government to entrepreneurs, Korea has been transformed from a less developed country into a developing country and then into a semi-developed country. In becoming a developed country, wages will inevitably be raised until they meet the marginal cost of capital needed to automate production processes, and, as democracy develops, government cannot so definitively promote certain industries at the expense of others. Korean companies cannot compete with counterparts from advanced nations by venturing into risky investments, because increased competition has lowered industry-wide marginal profits and major losses are more likely. So, if Korea is to become an advanced nation, professional managers and engineers must have a prominent role, yet workers too will have to cooperate with efforts to improve productivity. The government needs to stabilise the business environment so that planning can be conducted with greater certainty, and entrepreneurs and powerful family-business groups must bestow responsibilities and authority on corporate managers.

Implications for Other Nations

This analysis has indicated the roles which workers, politicians and technocrats, entrepreneurs, and professional managers and engineers must perform if international competitiveness is to be strengthened. Industries at an early stage of development need to invest in endowed resources; those at a growth stage must improve the business environment; those at a maturing stage must build synergy with related and supporting industries. Governments should determine their policies towards different industries based on the proper understanding of their level of international competitiveness. A comprehensive industrial policy should reinforce mutually supportive links between industries, but governments should appreciate when its active engagement is desirable and when it becomes less beneficial. Entrepreneurs, professional managers and engineers should also appreciate their varying roles in an industry's life cycle, and the organisation of firms and the setting of policy have to adjust.

Limitations of the Study and Suggestions for Future Research

This research attempted to analyse the international competitiveness of a nation from static and dynamic perspectives, by using the nine-factor and the life cycle models. Caution is needed in the generalising of the nine-factor model because it has only been to Korea and the industrial life cycle approach has been tested against four Korean industries. The findings in this study need to be validated by similar and parallel work on other nations and industries.

NOTES

1. M.E. Porter, 'The Competitive Advantage of Nations', *Harvard Business Review* (March–April 1990), pp.84–5.
2. C. Brown and T.D. Sheriff, 'De-industrialization: A Background Paper, in F. Blackaby (ed.), *De-industrialization* (London: Heinemann, 1978).
3. HMSO, Report from the Select Committee of the House of Lords on Overseas Trade, The Aldington Report, 1985.
4. A. Francis and P.K.M. Tharakan (eds.), *The Competitiveness of European Industry* (London and NY: Routledge, 1989), pp.5–20.
5. M.J. Baker and Susan J. Hart, *Marketing and Competitive Success* (Philip Allan, 1989), pp.5–8.
6. W. Leontief, 'Factor Proportions and Structure of American Trade: Further Theoretical and Empirical Analysis', *Review of Economics and Statistics*, Vol.38.
7. C.P. Kindleberger, *American Business Abroad* (New Haven: Yale University Press, 1969), p.13.
8. P.J. Buckley and M. Casson, *The Future of the Multinational Enterprise* (MacMillan, 1976), pp.33–65.
9. See J.H. Dunning, *International Production and the Multinational Enterprise* (London: George Allen & Unwin, 1981), Table 4.2 'The Eclectic Theory of International Production', on pp.80–81, and Ch.5, 'Explaining the International Direct Investment Position of Countries: Towards a Dynamic or Developmental Approach', on pp.109–37. See also J.H. Dunning, *Explaining International Production* (London: Unwin Hyman Ltd., 1988), Ch.5, 'The Investment Development Cycle and Third World Multinationals', pp.140–65.
10. P.J. Buckley and M.C. Casson, Ch.2, 'Multinational Enterprises in Less Developed Countries: Cultural and Economic Interactions', in P.J. Buckley and J. Clegg (eds.), *Multinational Enterprises in Less Developed Countries* (London: MacMillan, 1991), pp.27–55.
11. B. Kogut, 'Designing Global Strategies: Comparative and Competitive Value-Added Chains', *Sloan Management Review* (Summer 1985), pp.15–28; W. Goldsmith and D. Clutterbuck, *The Winning Streak: Britain's Top Companies Reveal Their Formulas for Success* (Weidenfeld & Nicolson, 1984); I. Yamazawa, 'Intensity Analysis of World Trade Flow', *Hitotsubashi Journal of Economics* (1970), pp.61–90.

12. M.E. Porter, *The Comparative Advantage of Nations* (NY: The Free Press, 1990), pp.69–130.
13. Uh Sun Shin, *Resource Economics* (Park-Young Sa, 1988), pp.9–11.
14. M.E. Porter, op. cit., pp.107–24.
15. Ibid., pp.100–06.
16. Ibid., pp.86–100.
17. The per capita GNP standard measuring each nation's economic status differs from one scholar to another. In this research, the standards dividing less-developed nations, developing nations, semi-developed nations and developed nations were set at US$500, US$3,000 and US$15,000. Please refer to W.J. Keegan, *Global Marketing Management* (4th edn., Englewood Cliffs, NJ: Prentice-Hall, 1989), pp.86–9 for further details.
18. Please refer to J.E. Smallwood, 'The Product Life Cycle: A Key to Strategic Marketing Planning', in B.A. Weitz and R. Wensley (ed.), *Strategic Marketing: Planning Implementation and Control* (Boston, MA: Kent Publishing Company, 1984), pp.184–92 for further details.
19. Japanese shipbuilding industry provides an example. Japanese shipbuilding industry fell into a declining stage in the early 1980s due in the main to the cost leadership possessed by developing countries such as Korea and Brazil. Since the mid-1980s, however, Japan has drastically changed the nature of the industry by introducing robotisation into manufacturing processes, thereby recovering their cost competitiveness.
20. Korea Electronic Industries Promotion Institute, 'Prospect for Long-term Development of Electronic Industries', 1989. 9.
21. KIET, 'Future Picture of Automobile Industries', Series of Future Industries, 1987.
22. Hanil Synthetic Fiber Co. Ltd. lost the title of general trading company in 1981.

The Competitive Advantage of Japanese Industries: Developments, Dimensions and Directions

YOSHITAKA SUZUKI

INTRODUCTION

This article assesses the validity of Michael Porter's framework in explaining Japanese industrial development. It asks a number of essential questions. First, to what extent do the facts dealt with in his work illustrate the main processes of Japanese industrial development? Second, does Japanese advantage rest on the truly systemic management of a 'value chain' which incorporates suppliers, producers, distributors and supportive sectors? Third, to what degree can product differentiation be a major source of competitive advantage for Japanese firms? On the first question Porter uses a data-set which leads him to exaggerate the competitive advantages of Japanese industry. On the second, we can find a value chain system in every field of the Japanese economy, but it only worked effectively in particular industries such as processing and fabrication, and the relationship to success in world export markets is far from axiomatic. Regarding the third, critical examples of product differentiation can be discovered in Porter's data-set for many Japanese industries, especially in consumer end-products, but it did not necessarily create Japan's national competitive advantage.

PORTER ON JAPAN

In *The Competitive Advantage of Nations*, Michael Porter attempts to establish a theoretical framework through the careful observation of various and extensive facts and, by this inductive method, he seeks to explain the international competitiveness of firms. First, Porter emphasises how the advantages of product differentiation are as important as those achieved by lower cost. Second, successful industrial clusters are, according to his explanation, brought forth by the interactions of several determinants, most notably factor conditions, demand conditions, related and supporting industries, and inter-firm rivalry, and they are in effect a value chain in which the process of economic activity is organised. Third, he proposes a model of national competitive development, based on the experiences of many countries, in which differentiation plays a decisive

---

Yoshitaka Suzuki, Tohoku University

role. Porter's work clearly shows how a value chain system and the practice of product differentiation are developed. The affinity between his theoretical framework and empirical facts is highly evidenced through the comparative observation of many nations. Porter examines each of the determinants of competitive advantage enjoyed by Japanese industries. He characterises them in turn as the 'rapid upgrading of factors of production', 'demanding buyers', 'cooperative suppliers', and 'aggressive domestic rivalry', and he concludes that Japanese industry presents the most lucid and successful example of the determinants of national competitive advantage working as a system.[1] In making such a statement, there seems to be no critical misunderstanding of the facts; the purpose of his work is not to produce new data, but to test his framework against existing empirical evidence. He does, correctly, question existing explanations which tend to over-emphasise the role of government, or the mystical characteristics of 'Japanese management', which must after all exist in both successful and less successful industries. Some of his points require further examination. First, how was the Japanese value chain system so praised by Porter formed by the interactions of factor and created endowments and other determinants? Second, to what extent do the factors presented in his work represent the main process of Japanese industrial development? Third, why is Japanese competitive advantage truly systemic, and why is there a large group of industries in Japan that is sheltered from competition? Fourth, to what degree has differentiation been a major source of competitive advantage for Japanese firms? In some of these points, further discussion is necessary but, in other cases, an alternative explanation may be more appropriate. We will cover each of these points, and examine how far Porter's framework can be used to interpret Japanese industrial development.

DEVELOPMENT: JAPANESE COMPETITIVE ADVANTAGE

Porter sees his task as the need 'to explain the pattern of success and failure in . . . industries and how this has been changing over time', and the necessity of understanding the formation of a value chain in particular Japanese industries. In dealing with Japan, his explanation often seems rhetorical, a manner quite different from his careful analysis in earlier parts of the book. For instance, all the determinants are qualified by superlatives: 'demand conditions prove to be one of *the most important of the determinants* of national competitive advantage in Japanese industry';[2] 'the role of related and supporting industries in Japanese national competitive advantage is among *the most striking aspects* of the Japanese economy';[3] and 'perhaps *the single greatest determinant* of Japanese success . . . is the nature of domestic rivalry'[4] (the emphasis is mine). This type of analysis makes it difficult to judge the interactions and importance of the determinants of success within the industrial system. In addition to the basic analytical approach, the data presented only partially shows the process of Japanese industrial development. Porter's argument is based on 1985 data, compiled from the United Nations' *Yearbook of International Trade Statistics*. This publication has provided valuable statistics since 1971, and is one of the best sources for a comprehensive comparison like Porter's. He uses 1971 data for the United States and other post-war winners, but 1985 (and partly 1978) data for Japan and other emerging nations during the 1970s and 1980s. As Japanese industries have to a large extent depended on manufacturing and on export rather than overseas investment in global development and competition, *International Statistics* is a useful source by which to assess the performance of Japanese firms.

Porter lists the top 50 Japanese industries in terms of their share of world exports in 1985. Table 1, by contrast, lists all Japanese industries which have at various points in time possessed competitive advantage relative to world-wide competitors. All those Japanese industries that were either the world's largest exporter in each trade or had more than 20 per cent of world exports have been selected. Table 1 will allow us to assess the position of individual Japanese industries and Japanese industry as a whole at each specified date. It also indicates fluctuating fortunes or, in other words, 'the pattern of success and failure in . . . industries and how this has been changing over time'. Table 1 shows that 1985 was an extraordinary peak for Japanese exports, which, to be exact, lasted for a few years. The number of industries in which Japan possesses competitive advantage decreased from 83 to 56 between 1985 and 1990. Although most of Porter's 'top 50 Japanese industries in 1985' continued to remain in Table 1 after 1985, their shares in world export declined significantly during the last few years of the 1980s. The year 1985 stands out prominently in the history of Japanese industry both in terms of competitive industries and their shares of world trade. As Japan had 58 such industries in 1978, it means that within two to three years Japan had lost a position which had taken more than seven years to achieve.

It is doubtful whether a sample which experienced a rapid regression just after the peak which it quotes is adequate for a discussion of sustained competitive advantage. These changes have been credited to a rapid rise in the strength of the yen, the relative progress of newly industrialising and other developing countries, and a shift from domestic to foreign investment by some Japanese industries. These factors, the loss of competitive advantage either through exchange rates or by cost, were not regarded as essential in Porter's discussion. There are time differentials between peak and decline in those industries which had competitive advantage in 1985. Some industries in consumer end-products lost their position before the dramatic rise of the yen, just as those in fabricated basic materials came to a climax in 1985 and rapidly declined after that.

TABLE 1

JAPANESE PRODUCTS WHICH POSSESSED THE LARGEST OR MORE
THAN 20 PER CENT OF WORLD EXPORTS IN EACH INDUSTRY, 1964-90
(PERCENTAGE IN EACH YEAR)

	1964	1971	1978	1985	1990
Fish, prepared or preserved	42.6	37.1	20.4	15.2	---
Synthetic fibres	21.3	19.8	---	---	---
Other man-made fibres	---	20.6	20.5	---	---
Nitrogenous-function compounds	27.3	38.2	---	---	---
Chemical nitrogenous fertilisers	15.6	11.0	---	---	---
Rubber tyres, bus or lorry	---	---	28.9	39.1	24.1
Continuous synthetic fibre yarn	---	---	---	25.5	---
Textile fibre yarn	12.0	14.2	---	---	---
Woven cotton fabrics	29.6	14.6	---	---	---
Woven synthetic fabrics	38.7	44.2	42.4	34.7	---
Woven regenerated fabrics	27.1	---	---	21.0	---
Cement	---	10.3	17.1	14.0	---
Pottery	36.2	34.8	27.6	27.7	---
Pig iron, spiegeleisen, etc.	---	---	---	21.4	---
Iron and steel, coils	25.8	29.4	28.6	---	---
Iron and steel, wire rods	---	21.8	27.0	22.1	---
Iron and steel, bars	---	---	18.5	19.1	---
Iron and steel, profiles	---	---	---	20.5	---
Iron and steel, heavy plates	---	34.9	28.4	22.7	---
Iron and steel, medium plates	---	48.4	27.7	19.6	---
Iron and steel, thin uncoated	23.1	34.2	38.5	32.2	20.1
Tinned plates	---	28.8	27.6	29.3	19.2
Iron and steel, thin coated	29.8	42.0	34.8	27.9	18.1
Railway rails	---	---	---	25.0	13.0
Iron and steel, wires	22.9	24.7	---	16.5	---
Iron and steel, tubes, seamless	---	23.8	35.1	38.7	27.4
Iron and steel, tubes and pipes	27.2	35.9	35.3	20.6	---
Iron and steel, tube fittings	---	---	18.2	---	---
Wire ropes	---	23.8	24.5	21.6	---
Steel and copper nails	36.6	22.9	23.7	24.2	---
Cutlery	---	25.0	21.7	22.5	---
Iron and steel chains	---	---	20.9	21.8	20.8
Steam boilers	---	---	---	19.0	13.7
Steam engines	---	---	25.6	20.1	23.2
Motor vehicle pistons	---	---	---	---	17.6
Marine piston engines	---	---	25.9	37.1	30.0
Piston engines	---	---	---	---	23.0
AC meters	---	---	23.6	23.4	19.3
Sewing machines	29.3	33.5	31.7	35.4	34.6
Spinning machines	---	---	---	---	22.9
Weaving machines	---	---	---	21.3	25.9
Metal working machine-tools	---	---	---	32.8	22.2
Metal working machinery	---	---	---	25.6	---
Rolling mills	---	---	---	29.8	---
Industrial furnaces	---	---	22.5	---	---
Air conditioning machinery	---	---	---	29.6	23.1
Centrifugal pumps	---	---	---	21.8	---
Pumps for gases	---	---	---	24.1	22.6
Fork lifts	---	---	18.3	29.9	21.1
Nonelectric power tools	---	---	---	---	20.7
Ball and roller bearings	---	---	---	20.3	---
Typewriters	---	---	---	38.1	23.8
Calculators	---	---	49.6	66.8	37.8
Photocopying apparatus	---	---	44.2	65.9	42.6
Data-processor peripherals	---	---	---	37.9	25.2
Track-laying tractors	---	---	42.1	51.8	28.2
Self-propelled bulldozers	---	---	---	50.6	35.0

THE COMPETITIVE ADVANTAGE OF JAPANESE INDUSTRIES   41

TABLE 1 (cont)

	1964	1971	1978	1985	1990
Self-propelled shovels	---	---	---	38.4	24.4
Heating and cooling equipment	---	---	---	18.1	---
Television receivers	34.4	49.4	31.8	49.5	---
Radio receivers	53.1	61.3	54.8	45.6	24.1
Sound recorders	23.0	48.1	58.3	77.2	58.2
Line telephone equipment	---	---	---	26.2	28.6
Microphones and loudspeakers	---	---	41.4	56.8	30.9
Telecommunications equipment	---	31.5	45.2	55.7	27.4
TV and radio transmitters	---	---	26.1	29.8	20.0
Electrical transformers	---	---	21.4	22.8	14.9
Static converters	---	---	---	28.3	---
Fixed variable resistors	---	---	20.4	24.5	32.7
Electric insulating equipment	22.7	---	24.0	29.7	22.7
Electro-medical equipment	---	---	---	20.4	25.0
Household refrigerators	---	---	---	21.2	---
TV picture tubes	---	---	36.1	42.4	24.4
Other electronic tubes	---	---	20.9	36.5	60.3
Electronic microcircuits	---	---	---	22.2	---
Batteries	---	---	---	17.6	19.2
Automotive electric equipment	---	---	---	25.4	22.1
Electro-mechanical hand tools	---	---	---	25.0	---
Transistors and valves	---	---	---	21.2	22.3
Electrical condensers	---	19.7	24.1	27.5	30.7
Electrical carbons	---	24.0	23.1	24.1	---
Motor vehicles	---	---	22.6	30.7	24.8
Lorries	---	---	28.2	37.5	25.2
Buses	---	21.7	22.8	38.7	20.5
Motor vehicle chassis	---	---	---	---	23.5
Motor cycles	52.4	72.3	75.0	82.0	58.8
Bicycles	---	25.6	35.9	---	---
Ships	36.6	41.5	44.5	31.4	28.2
Boats and vessels	27.6	29.6	33.1	37.3	15.2
Textile clothes, not knitted	18.1	---	---	---	---
Textile clothing, not knitted	28.6	---	---	---	---
Optical elements	29.4	42.7	55.3	42.8	42.5
Cameras	34.1	30.2	53.3	62.2	50.8
Cinema cameras and projectors	---	---	37.1	---	---
Photo and cinema supplies	---	---	---	21.9	22.4
Watches and movements	---	---	23.6	25.7	---
Clocks	---	---	21.0	26.9	---
Musical instruments	21.4	35.6	23.0	34.7	---
Combustible products	---	---	26.6	23.8	17.2
Smallwares, toiletry	---	---	32.7	23.8	---
Toys	30.6	21.8	---	---	---
Outdoor sporting goods	25.6	---	---	---	---
Pens and pencils	---	---	---	28.9	21.5

Sources: 1964: estimated from *1964 World Trade Annual*; 1964, 1971, 1978, 1985 and 1990. United Nations, *Yearbook of International Trade statistics, 1964–90*.

On the other hand, some industries in producer end-products, such as industrial machinery and their components, have maintained their competitive positions well after 1985.

In Porter's discussion, 'clusters', those mutually strengthening linkages within a nation's competitive industries, play an important role in creating the competitive advantage of a nation. His analysis seems to suggest that recent Japanese success resulted from the formation of mutually supportive industrial clusters which have established linked value chains of economic activity and competitive advantages based mainly on product differentiation. As we have seen, this particular combination of factors may only be especially true of the mid-1980s, and the statistics of prior and later years might well lead to different conclusions. Table 2, therefore, is an attempt to give Japanese industrial clusters relative weight over time in proportion to their share of world exports by combining the various competitive industries of each period into groups. It is possible to obtain data for 1964 and 1971 if we follow Porter's seven year indent. Although the *Yearbook of International Trade Statistics* does not provide the export shares of each product or nation in 1964, the necessary data can be unearthed in other sources. Table 2, however, is not able to show directly the relationship between groups of industries. For the period before 1970, it is difficult to find clusters which form the basis of Japanese competitive advantage. Japan's exports reached their pre-World War II level, on a dollar basis, in 1964, but her foreign trade was still in deficit.[5] Japanese products which could compete effectively in the world market before 1970 were to be found in textiles, fertilisers, food and other daily necessities. The position of all these products diminished in world markets by the mid-1970s. For the period before 1964, the ratio of each Japanese product in terms of total world exports is not known. Japanese exports were, in the main, composed of the same products as those listed in 1964, and some traditional goods, in which Japan had more than 20 per cent of total exports in 1964, are to be found in the 1971 list. But new groups of products were appearing and their shares grew rapidly in the latter half of the 1970s. Some industries such as iron and steel experienced two peaks: for some basic steel products the peak had already passed, while for new products the peak was yet to arrive. The Japanese industries that were competitive in the world markets of 1971 were, in many cases, independently organised areas of production, and they did not demonstrate mutually supportive interdependence or competitively enhancing linkages. Neither a wide range of clusters nor intricate value chains were observable among competitive industries before 1970. The facts suggest, according to Porter's framework, that the competitive advantage of these industries was based on a lead in costs. To put it more directly, it was based on low labour costs. In these groups of industries, the decline of their exports after 1985 was accompanied by an increase in overseas direct investment by steel companies. Following the two peaks in Japanese steel exports, there were two subsequent climaxes in overseas investment by the steel companies.

On the other hand, Porter's analysis of industries in which Japan did have a competitive advantage in 1985 can be reaffirmed. That is, Japanese competitive advantage can be discovered in groups of industries such as high-grade steel, industrial machinery, electric equipment,

TABLE 2

JAPANESE INDUSTRIAL CLUSTERS, 1964, 1971, 1978, 1985 and 1990

		Food	Textiles	Chemicals	Paper and ceramics	Iron and steel	Industrial machinery	Electrical equipments	Automobiles	Precision machinery	Others	Total
Consumer end-products	1990							111	84	116	38	349
	85	43			28	23		220	113	214	77	718
	78	37			28	22		145	134	213	59	638
	71	20			35	25		159	98	109	22	468
	64	15	72		36			111	52	85	31	402
Producer end-products	1990						580	196	46			822
	85						786	318	76			1180
	78						361	179	51			591
	71			49			105	32	22			208
	64			43			94	23				160
Semi-finished products	1990				24	21		157				202
	85		81		39	68	20	192	24			424
	78		42	21	29	87		104				283
	71		73	40		47		44				204
	64		107	21		37						165
Fabricated basic materials	1990					98						98
	85				14	315						329
	78				17	235						252
	71				10	324						334
	64					129						129
Total	1990				24	119	580	464	130	116	38	1471
	85	43	81		81	406	806	730	213	214	77	2651
	78	37	42	21	74	344	361	428	185	213	59	1764
	71	20	73	89	45	396	105	235	120	109	22	1214
	64	15	179	64	36	166	94	134	52	85	31	856

Note: The numbers are a sum total of percentages of world export of each product which belong to each industry. They simply indicate the relative weight of each cluster.

transportation machinery, and precision machinery. These sectors rely upon intricate supply and demand relationships, namely 'clusters', among these industries. First, household electric equipment and shipbuilding had established their position in the world market by the mid-1960s, and they had a 'pull' effect on the steel and precision machinery industries. Then, competitive advantage shifted to industrial machinery, and its supplier, high-grade steel. Growth in industrial machinery was the result of diversification strategies amongst companies in shipbuilding, precision machinery, and electric equipment, while growth in high-grade steel stemmed from the differentiation policies of integrated steel companies. Japanese steel firms obtained capabilities by which they upgraded and met new demands in automobile supplies, household electrics, industrial machinery, electronics, and building materials. Most of the products in which Japan gained advantage after the 1970s were based on the management of value chains in identifiable industrial clusters. In textiles and seafood, where Japan was losing its competitive position, developing countries achieved lower production costs and began to undermine previously established rivals. Before long, Japan was importing these products. Industries in which Japan gained competitive power after the 1970s required related industries for their development, and the mere introduction of new technology providing lower labour costs would not have brought competitive advantage.

This new group of industries belonged to processing, fabrication and related industries. These enjoyed lower production costs by making use of extended value chains which enable the flow of goods to be efficiently coordinated. The role of the value chain was realised as firms built upon cost advantages already won. The rise and decline of a series of industries from 1970 to the mid-1980s can be understood in terms of a shift of competition from lower production costs as a consequence of labour factors to that of lower costs gained through value chains, not necessarily as a shift from factor cost advantage to product differentiation. A decline in the advantage once held by Japanese processing and fabrication industries after the mid-1980s suggests that their cost and value chain advantages could not compensate for rising exchange rates. The relative price of goods from emerging competitors was demonstrated to be critical. The last two or three years of the 1980s, when Japanese exports of these products rapidly declined, also saw an increase of overseas direct investment by processing and fabrication companies.[6]

DIMENSIONS: THE UNIVERSAL VALIDITY OF PORTER'S FRAMEWORK

The third question concerns the relationship between Porter's theoretical framework and the facts which are explained by this framework or, in other words, the scope of validity inherent in Porter's explanation. Porter states that 'Japanese advantage is truly systemic . . .'. In fact, only a limited group of Japanese industries had a sustainable competitive advantage. All of those quoted by Porter can be found in the processing and fabrication industries while, in other manufacturing industries such as chemicals, oil, paper, food, and in almost all non-manufacturing industries, Japan has had no competitive advantage, even after the 1970s. The particular strengths of processing and fabrication, which were pointed out by Porter, can be ascertained in Table 2. Why does Japan have competitive advantage in some industries and not in others? Is it possible for those industries which possess no competitive advantage to obtain it if they produce similar value chain systems? Or is it that, in spite of the existence of a similar system in these industries, they cannot be competitive because of government protection and regulations? Porter seems to suggest this possibility. However, it is not easy to establish cause and effect between government protection and a lack of competitive advantage.

Regarding the affinity between Porter's 'system' and particular industry characteristics, it is possible to find a commonality between his work and those industries in which Japan had a clear competitive advantage. Almost all of them, as we have noted, belong to processing, fabrication, and their supplying branches. In comparison to many industries, they are multi-assembly operations, and productivity and costs are determined by the efficiency with which parts are supplied. Competitive power depends on how efficiently the flow of goods is coordinated or, in Porter's terms, how well a value chain is operated. In cases of product differentiation, complicated flows of goods have to be managed. Theoretically, the lengthy flow of goods from raw materials through processing to fabrication, so characteristic of these industries, can be coordinated in various ways. It is possible to internalise the whole process within a single firm. Some American automobile firms, for instance, have manufactured and supplied their own components.[7] By doing so, they reduce the uncertainty of market transactions. They can supply the necessary kinds and volumes of parts by making use of organisational structures located within their own firms. At the same time, however, such vertical integration does carry a cost in management, fixed investment and overheads, and this would be large in processing and fabrication industries simply because they have to internalise so many activities. Alternatively, a firm can make use of outside market mechanisms. If the market mechanism works efficiently, it can coordinate the flow of many thousands of parts, and reduce fixed capital investment, overheads and those other management costs which accompany vertical integration. For example, the British shipbuilding industry, which had once held competitive advantage over the world, enjoyed a well-organised division of labour between hundreds of suppliers and shipbuilders.[8] Shipbuilding companies were free to concentrate on their core process with minimum overheads, but supplier–buyer coordination necessitated a well-developed market mechanism. Yet it is not necessarily easy for these individual markets to adapt and react swiftly to changes in the standards of goods and technology. Which type of coordination is chosen depends on relative market development, and the decisive factor for competitive advantage in the processing and fabrication industries is how to secure the supply of parts and components efficiently.

The practice of 'long-term mutual transactions', widely observed in Japanese industries, is important. This practice is well known as 'affiliation', and it is found not only within manufacturing branches, but in commerce and finance. Thirty per cent of the total output of Japanese manufacturing industries, for example, was sold through their affiliated wholesale channels between 1967 and 1980.[9] There exists a close mutual transaction between manufacturing and sales companies. In financing, such a long-term mutual transaction has been pivotal. Bank loans have played an important part in the financing of Japanese industrial companies, and most large-scale industrial companies have continued to depend on a particular bank for an important ratio of their loans.[10] Similar practices can be observed in the relations between companies engaged in assembling and supplying. Assembly companies buy most of their parts outside the firm, and this method of supply is different from vertical integration. It is also different from the market transaction, which can be characterised as a free entry–exit relationship and as being coordinated and determined by price. In this case, continuous transactions and a mutual exchange of information are widely practised as well as being necessary. Porter's description is partly correct in this respect.[11] Yet it took a long time to develop this relationship between assemblers and suppliers, and the nature of their links have changed over time. It was only in the last phase of development that the assemblers began to invite the assistance of suppliers in the design of final products. On consumer end-products it should be added that large-scale producer companies have established similar long-term and permanent transactions with retailers.

Companies which are closely affiliated accumulate information about each other after a lengthy period of association. By sharing information and commercial objectives, they work in unison, or seemingly as the departments of a single company. But companies rarely own shares in their suppliers. Their relationship is predicated only upon the transaction of goods and acknowledged interdependence, and it is free from many types of management overheads and fixed costs. Buyer–supplier and transaction links can be observed in all aspects of Japanese industrial organisation. It has worked particularly effectively in processing and fabrication and where multi-assembly operations are commonplace. It is these industries which exhibit competitive advantage and it is only these which conform well to Porter's model.

DIFFERENTIATION: AN EFFECTIVE DIRECTION FOR JAPANESE FIRMS?

The fourth issue which arises from Porter's discussion of Japan is differentiation. When Porter refers to Japanese advantage as the most applicable case of his theoretical framework, it implies that the advantage is strong and continuing. This advantage, according to his analysis, stems from the product differentiation achieved by Japanese companies by the mid-1980s. Porter defines differentiation as 'the ability to provide unique and superior value to a buyer in terms of product quality, special features, or after-sale service'.[12] Expressed in these terms it has been sought by almost all Japanese industries making consumer end-products and examples are to be found in many individual companies. The essential question is whether such differentiation has contributed to the advantage of Japanese companies. The best cases of Japanese competitive advantage are evidenced by three prominent industries – transportation equipment, electrical machinery and industrial machinery. And differentiation has had mixed results for these groups, or even for firms within the same sector.

The first category, transportation equipment, contains the automobile industry. Leading motor vehicle companies have created a production system that allows them to manufacture the product quantities required by market demand. They possess the flexibility to allocate workers to different production lines, and can manufacture a variety of high quality products simultaneously. In the latter half of the 1980s, Japanese automobile companies extended their differentiation strategies, probably beyond the needs of the market, by adopting frequent model changes and by multiplying the number of lines available. The basic passenger car models produced by Japanese companies were 130 in 1978, 230 in 1985, and 380 in 1990. The amount of production of each basic type remained stable throughout the first half of the 1980s, although it had increased by some 20 per cent by the end of the decade.[13] Japanese automobile companies faced rising production costs and productivity declined through the latter half of the 1980s. Differentiation through small-batch production of many models did not lead to the successful expansion of markets.

In our second group, electrical machinery, household electrics and electronic devices have formed two important branches. Total sales of Japanese electrical and electronic products amounted to some 23 billion yen, a sum equal to that of automobiles. The household electric industry has traditionally been the major division within this sector. It grew rapidly until the early 1970s, since when stability and incremental increases have been the norm. In the face of a saturated domestic market, the sector pursued differentiation, seeking to convince consumers with new models and products. The basic types of colour television receivers made in Japan increased from 101 in 1968 to 213 in 1972. The number of sizes, six in 1968, rose to ten by 1972.[14] The 'compact, portable, quiet and multifunctional' products that Porter focuses on were unable to stimulate growth in the domestic market, nor were there linkages or benefits in export markets, where different lines were needed.[15] Differentiation is merely a subdivision of size, design, packaging, naming, and functions of what is essentially the same product. It is hard to see how in household electricals, as in automobiles, it helped to maintain Japanese competitive advantage. By the early 1980s, Japan had fallen below neighbouring Asian countries as the household electrical producing centre of the world, whilst overseas production by Japanese companies amounted to a quarter of their total output by 1990.

Throughout the 1980s, new product lines appeared alongside traditional household electric equipment. In 1990, Japanese companies making VCRs, video cameras, car stereo systems and air conditioning equipment controlled more than half of their world markets. CDs, cordless telephones, facsimile machines, family computers and wordprocessors, to which were applied compatible microelectronic technology, also demonstrated strong competitive positions.[16] In a broad sense, these products can, indeed, be regarded as the results of differentiation. But, compared to their predecessors, such as television sets or washing machines, each market was small and rapidly changing, and companies had continuously to consider how microelectronic technology might be used for new products. As far as electronic devices are concerned the consequences of differentiation have been somewhat different than was the case with household electrics. Japanese companies had a strong foothold in household electronics, but semiconductor devices have already overtaken these consumer goods in output terms. In the electronic devices industry technological change has been rapid and production equipment soon became outdated. Companies have consistently invested in complicated and expensive fixed equipment. In this sector the quality of goods has been improved and product types have risen in number with the development of minute-processing technology.

Industrial machinery, the third group, consists of two main branches, machine tools and general machinery.[17] In machine tools, Japanese companies succeeded in producing multi-purpose and small- to medium-scale lines by developing numerical control technology, which bestows high production quality and accuracy. However, the market is not large enough for more than 150 firms. Many of them made inroads into the design and production of 'machining centres', which integrate the functions of existing single-purpose tools and so meet the needs of flexible manufacturing systems. Due to the relatively small domestic market, export opportunities were vital and these grew rapidly in the years to

1990, accounting for a full 30 per cent of total production. Exports were first directed to the US, where they were altered to meet import regulations and local production requirements. When efforts were directed towards Europe, similar adjustments had to be made.

There was an extensive market for 'general machinery', the name given to equipment used in manufacturing and services. Japanese companies have maintained their competitive advantage in many of the sector's diversified products, although the market as a whole is not large. Most products are made to order, the process being dependent on a high interchangeability of parts and technology, and most Japanese companies make a wide variety of products. As entry barriers are low there is great difficulty in sustaining product differentiation. But it is in this branch of the industry that Japan has maintained a competitive advantage.

These three basic industry groups and their leading sub-branches displayed varying attitudes to differentiation. In automobiles and household electrics, differentiation was earnestly pursued, but it could not halt a decline in their competitive positions after 1985. Their markets in Japan were mature, and differentiation did not supply the answer. Excessive differentiation led to an increase in production costs, and eventually manufacturers were to reduce their product types. In industrial machinery, differentiation is difficult to achieve, and it cannot be used as a mainspring of competitive advantage. In each leading branch of the machinery groups, differentiation was not important in either the gaining or sustaining of competitive advantage.

There are some industries in which differentiation was comparatively influential, and Porter's analysis matches the evidence available. In electronic devices and machine tools, differentiation has been revealed as an effective means of competition. In steel, non-ferrous metals, and partly in chemicals, Japanese firms maintain competitive advantage with a limited range of products. Non-ferrous metals companies have supplied high-grade powder metals, electronic devices and materials to Japanese assembling and processing industries. Within the chemical industry, the plastics divisions have adjusted to the requirements of users by supplying more than 1,000 product types to automobile, electric equipment and building material companies. In most of these sectors exports, as a proportion of total sales, is still quite small and the competitive advantage that these sectors do possess is not demonstrated in Porter's data. In a few minor markets, differentiation by the mid-1980s was related to competitive advantage. In most cases, the connection with export success is tenuous.

CONCLUSION

Porter does not attribute the determinants of the competitive advantage of nations to any one particular factor, but to the existence of a system consisting of several of them. He argues that successful Japanese industries are part of a system in which competitive advantages are self-reinforcing. He never adequately explains how these systems might be formed. In contending that a cluster or a value chain system is created by an interaction of different factors it is hard to discern cause and effect relationships. A number of points need to be made. First, 1985 was a special year for the Japanese economy. Its especially strong competitive position was established within a short period of time, but collapsed after the mid-1980s in an even shorter one. These events cast some doubt on the extent to which Porter's evidence explains Japanese industrial development. We should be careful not to generalise about Japanese competitive advantage from over-dependence on the 1985 data alone. Second, it is indeed possible to see the workings of value chains and clusters in some Japanese industries since the late 1970s. Yet the main contribution of these value chains is to be found in the obtaining of cost advantage through the efficient co-ordination of the flow of goods in the production process.

Third, Porter lays particular stress on the systemic nature of Japanese advantage. Well-developed systems and links can be found in supplier–buyer transactions in Japan. Moreover, they exist not only in a purely goods-producing setting amongst both successful and not-so-successful firms, but in bank–industry relations, too. However, transaction-based systems may well work efficiently in the processing and fabrication industries which require a wide range of complicated parts. It is only these companies which possess the competitive advantage outlined in Porter's book. Fourth, differentiation was not always the main source of Japanese competitive advantage. Since the mid-1980s, Japanese industries have maintained their advantage in some smaller markets through differentiation, so long as differentiation proceeded simultaneously with cost reduction. Japan has since then lost large markets in spite of, and partly because of, differentiation. Japan also possesses competitive advantages in some industries which are sustained by strategies other than differentiation. Value chain systems and differentiation did not necessarily create competitive advantages for Japanese companies in 1985. In some important industries Japan shifted an advantage based on lower labour costs to another resting on lower transaction costs through a value chain which, in turn, is being undermined by new competitors.

NOTES

1. M. Porter, *The Competitive Advantage of Nations* (New York, 1990), pp.395, 418–20.
2. Ibid., p.401.
3. Ibid., p.406.
4. Ibid., p.411.
5. From the end of World War II until 1964, Japan recorded an enormous deficit in foreign trade. It first went into the black in 1965, and remained in balance between 1965 and

1970. After 1971 Japan's foreign trade improved remarkably and impressively and, at the same time, its foreign direct investments began to increase.
6. Japan External Trade Relations Organisation, *Annual Report of JETRO 1993* (Tokyo, 1993).
7. M. Matsui, *Jidosha Buhin* (Automobile Parts), (Tokyo, 1988).
8. S. Pollard, 'British and World Shipbuilding, 1890–1914: A Study in Comparative Costs', *Journal of Economic History*, Vol.17 (1957).
9. Y. Suzuki, *Japanese Management Structures 1920–80* (London, 1991), pp.95–7.
10. K. Okazaki, 'The Fund Raising Assistance Function of the "Main Banks"', *Annals of Economics*, Vol.55, No.2.
11. Porter, *Competitive Advantage*, pp.407–8.
12. Porter, *Competitive Advantage*, p.37. See also p.10.
13. Nihon Jidosha Kogyo-kai, *Japanese Automobile Industries*, (Tokyo, 1992); K. Shimokawa, 'Jidosha (Automobiles)', in S. Yonekawa and H. Yamazaki (eds.), *Sengo Nihon Keiei shi* (Business History of Post-War Japan), (Tokyo, 1990); K. Shimokawa, *Jidosha* (Automobiles), (Tokyo, 1991).
14. Ministry of International Trade and Industry, *Electronic Industries Yearbook 1975* (Tokyo, 1974), p.775. Sources by Professor A. Hiramoto.
15. Porter, *Competitive Advantage*, p.403.
16. Kaden Seihin Kyokai, *Handbook of Household Electric Industries, 1992* (Tokyo, 1992). See also argument by T. Iida in J. Takamura (ed.), *Gyotaibetsu Sangyo no Tenbo* (Perspectives of Individual Industries), (Tokyo, 1993).
17. Ministry of International Trade and Industry, *Statistical Yearbook of Mechanical Engineering, 1992* (Tokyo, 1991); Y. Omichi and A. Kawakita, 'Kosaku Kikai, Sangyo Kikai' (Mechanical Engineering and Industrial Machinery), in J. Takamura (ed.), *Gyotaibetsu Sangyo no Tenbu*.

Trade, Industry and Government: The Development of Organisational Capabilities in Singapore

SIOW-YUE CHIA

INTRODUCTION

There is a burgeoning literature seeking to explain the economic success of the Asian newly industrialising economies (NIEs). The latest is the World Bank study covering eight high-performing Asian economies, and it concluded that success was largely due to the adoption of policies that contribute to high rates of physical and human capital formation.[1] It found extensive government intervention in several countries and that the state has been central to their success. This paper adopts Porter's framework to examine the case of Singapore.[2] The Singapore experience is a case of limited resources and people being organised into a disciplined society and efficient economy, in which government and foreign multinational corporations (MNCs) play dominant roles and domestic private enterprises a lesser part. The state influences all four determinants of national competitive advantage, namly factor conditions, demand conditions, supporting and related industries, and firm strategy, structure and rivalry. Singapore has strength in created factor advantages and this has to compensate for weaknesses in other areas. The strategic economic plan aims to upgrade the economy from the factor-driven stage to the investment- and innovation-driven stages; from a reliance on cost advantage and foreign technology towards product differentiation and the development of domestic expertise and know-how.[3]

SINGAPORE'S ECONOMIC PERFORMANCE

Some Performance Indicators

When Singapore achieved self-rule in May 1959 and independence in August 1965, there was deep concern over the economic viability of a small city-state. The People's Action Party (PAP) government had inherited an economy that faced severe problems – a lack of growth and a viable economic base, a population explosion, high unemployment, a labour force with limited education and skills, a militant trade union movement, and a social environment plagued by inadequate housing,

Siow-Yue Chia, National University of Singapore

health and education facilities. The government took to the tasks of nation building, economic revival, and the formation of a discplined population and workforce. It gave priority to economic development; controlled population growth; pursued prudent monetary and fiscal policies; and adopted an outward-looking development strategy, with an emphasis on export manufacturing and foreign direct investment at a time when the conventional wisdom was to foster import substitution and distrust MNCs.

Within a decade, Singapore had demonstrated its economic resilience, and soon afterwards emerged as an NIE and a model of economic development. Table 1 shows some economic performance indicators, and

TABLE 1
SINGAPORE ECONOMY – BASIC INDICATORS, 1960–92

	1960	1970	1980	1992
Population (million)	1.6	2.1	2.3	2.8
GNP: current prices (S$billion)	2.2	5.9	2.4	7.6
GDP: annual real growth rate (%)	na	8.7	9.4	6.9
Per capita GNP: current prices (S$000)	1.3	2.8	9.9	24.0
annual real growth rate (%)		6.7	8.0	5.1
	na			
GDP structure: (curent prices,% share)				
Agriculture & fishing	3.5	2.3	1.3	0.2
Manufacturing	11.4	20.0	29.1	27.9
Services	76.4	66.8	64.5	66.9
Commerce	32.1	27.1	21.7	15.9
Transport & communications	13.3	10.6	14.0	13.7
Financial & business services	14.0	16.4	19.7	27.0
Other services	17.0	12.7	9.1	10.4
Unemployment rate (%)	na	6.0	3.0	2.7
Gross national savings/GNP (%)	-2.4	19.3	34.2	46.4
Gross fixed capital formation/GNP (%)	9.4	32.2	42.2	39.8
Annual change in consumer price index (%)		1.2	5.6	2.7
Exchange rate (per US$)	na	3.1	2.1	1.6
Merchandise trade: (S$billion)				
Trade balance	-0.5	-2.6	-9.0	-8.0
Imports	3.5	7.0	48.0	108.3
Exports	3.0	4.4	39.0	100.3
Domestic exports (% share)	6.2	38.5	62.3	64.2
Entrepot exports (% share)	93.8	61.5	37.7	35.8
Services trade: (S$billion)				
Trade balance	0.3	0.9	5.9	13.8
Imports	0.3	0.8	9.2	28.9
Exports	0.7	1.7	15.1	42.7
Tourist arrivals (million)	0.09	0.5	2.6	6.0
Asian Currency Units' assets (US$billion)	-	0.4	5.4	35.5
Current account balance (S$billion)	-0.2	-1.7	-3.3	4.8
Official foreign reserves (S$billion)	na	3.1	13.8	65.8

Source: Ministry of Trade and Industry, *Economic Survey of Singapore 1992* (Singapore, 1993)
Note: Growth rates refer to 1960–70, 1970–80, 1980–92.

a number of achievements are highlighted. First, growth, has been rapid and sustained over three decades, with the increase in GDP averaging 8.3 per cent a year. Second, income growth has been accompanied by rapid labour absorption; from an unemployment rate of over ten per cent in the early 1960s, Singapore reached full employment in the early 1970s, becoming heavily dependent on foreign workers which form some 10–15 per cent of the labour force. Third, living standards improved. Per capita GNP grew at 6.5 per cent a year in real terms to reach US$14,714 by 1992. Singapore's per capita income is 17th in world rankings, and is second only to Japan in Asia. If adjusted for purchasing power, per capita income reached 71.2 per cent of the US level. During 1980–90, the average monthly household income of the bottom 20 per cent improved by more than six per cent a year in real terms. Low-cost public housing built since 1960 shelters 87 per cent of the population, and the home ownership rate stands at 82 per cent. Despite industrialisation and urbanisation, Singapore remains a green and clean city, with a low crime rate and efficient public services. Fourth, price stability was maintained despite rapid economic growth, with the consumer price index rising at less than an average three per cent a year in the past three decades. Fifth, savings rates have exceeded 45 per cent of GNP in recent years, and investment rates are among the highest in the world. The public external debt is negligible, and overseas assets have increased rapidly. By 1992, official foreign reserves reached US$40.4 billion or US$14,320 on a per capita basis.

Structural Transformation

Being a city-state with a manufacturing service base, Singapore has an atypical economic structure. Manufacturing accounted for 27.9 per cent of GDP in 1992, while services were responsible for 66.9 per cent. Of the latter, financial and business services led with 27.0 per cent, followed by commerce (15.9 per cent), transport and communications (13.7 per cent) and other services (10.4 per cent).

(i) From Entrepot to Manufacturing

The traditional economic pillars of Singapore, its entrepot and British military base, were respectively threatened by the growth of direct trading by neighbouring countries and Britain's wish to close down its colonial outpost. Industrialisation was needed as the new engine of growth.[4] But small size and a lack of natural resources, including water and energy, were unfavourable initial conditions. The land area was less than 600 square km and the population fewer than two million. The small domestic market precluded industries which operated with scale economies, and, as entrepot activities brought wage levels well above those characteristic of pre-industrial economies, Singapore had no competitive advantage in labour-intensive manufacturing. Singapore was not without advantages which encouraged industrialisation. It had a strategic geographical location with a natural harbour and an excellent transportation and communications infrastructure, which facilitated access to raw materials and markets. Location was to become a crucial factor for many industries and services. Singapore was not burdened by a lagging, low-productivity rural sector, and the transformation of a trading economy into an industrial economy was less daunting than the establishment of manufacturing against an agricultural background. It embarked on industrialisation from a fairly high level of economic development and standard of living; the labour force was literate and educated by the standards of colonial societies; and there was a substantial accumulation of capital resources and trading expertise. The long trading tradition contributed towards an outward-looking mind-set and a responsiveness to external changes. Singapore inherited an efficient state administration, run with high ethical standards, and this contributed to the cause of economic management in later years. Singapore's industrialisation strategy was originally dependent on policies of import substitution within the Malaysian common market, but the attainment of political independence in 1965 led to a labour-intensive, export-orientated and foreign-investment-led industrialisation strategy. The rapidity of subsequent economic growth and the ensuing labour shortage induced further restructuring of the economy through up-grading and the reduction of labour intensity.

Traditional industries in Singapore were of three types. There were the raw material processing industries which grew from the entrepot trade, and geographical location, a well-developed transport and communications network, and commercial and financial facilities led to Singapore's emergence as a processing centre for Southeast Asian rubber, tin, timber, vegetable oils, and other tropical produce destined for markets in North America, western Europe and Japan. This competitive advantage could not be sustained in later years because neighbouring countries began to create their own processing facilities. There were the ancillary engineering and ship-repair workshops that were part of Singapore's heritage as a major port and British naval base. There was the production of consumer goods and services for the domestic market, and these were protected from import competition by high transportation costs (furniture and construction materials) and perishability (food processing and beverages), as well as the relationship between proximity to customers and the effective delivery of a service (printing and publishing, and the repair of machinery and motor vehicles). Singapore's industry mix reveals the large share of intermediate and capital goods industries, which follows from the lack of emphasis on import substitution in consumer goods and from the city-state's development as a leading base for petroleum refining, ship-repairing, and a production base for MNCs in electronics. By the 1970s, Singapore had become the leading petroleum refining centre with a capacity of 1.1 billion barrels per day, with crude mostly imported from the Middle East. Four of the five refineries were fully foreign-owned – the companies of Shell, Esso and Mobil were prominent – while the fifth was a joint venture between the government, Caltex and British Petroleum. Singapore possesses large bunkering activities and its refineries supplied countries and companies in Asia-Pacific. The sourcing of crude was switched to Indonesia and Malaysia when Middle East supplies became uncertain in the 1970s. When new refineries came onstream in the Middle East and in neighbouring countries during the 1980s, the Singapore refineries decided to upgrade operations: efficiency and flexiblity was improved, contract processing for Asian crude suppliers was undertaken, and integration with the local petrochemical complex which emerged in the 1970s was pursued, Singapore's position as a centre for oil trading, distribution and storage being consequently enhanced.[5]

There was an influx of American MNCs in electronics assembly and the production of low-end components for export following an investment mission to the US in 1967 that promoted Singapore as an offshore manufacturing base. European and Japanese MNCs soon followed. The electronics industry has been subject to continuous upgrading, and, by the mid-1980s, it had restructured considerably, moving away from labour-intensive products and processes in response to changes in domestic factor endowments and cost competitiveness. Strengths included the use of surface mount technology and the production of high-density disk-drives, high-resolution graphic controllers, word processors, and components such as DRAMS and multi-layer PCBs. The industry is shifting towards the production of computers, including peripherals and components, and low value-added goods and processes have been phased out and transferred to neighbouring countries with abundant labour and lower wages. A large local and supporting industry making computer components, parts and supplies has emerged, facilitated by a growing pool of engineering expertise. Many MNCs have established international purchasing offices to source local and regional products for their worldwide requirements, and the government is directly encouraging the software industry as part of its information technology plan and as a complement to hardware manufacture.[6] Singapore's transport equipment industry is dominated by shipyards engaged mainly in ship repair and, to a lesser extent, the building of boats and oil rigs, as well as aircraft servicing and components manufacture. Singapore's role as a major shipping node, regional port, and one-time British naval base is well understood. Unlike the other major industries where foreign MNCs are dominant, the major shipyards are local enterprises which grew from the British naval dockyards that were converted in the late 1960s, and they are partially state-owned. The industry expanded into oil-rig construction in the 1970s in response to active exploration activities in Southeast Asian waters. Singapore is now a major regional aviation repair and overhaul centre and a manufacturing base for aircraft engine parts and components, exploiting its strategic location at the cross-roads of major international air routes. There is no motor vehicle assembly, and an automotive components sector has emerged through its links with the electronics industry, Singapore's infrastructure assisting efficient, timely and low-cost delivery to purchasers.

(ii) Growth of Services

In addition to manufacturing, Singapore's economic strategy has focused on the development of export services, and it is a regional financial, transport and telecommunications centre and a tourist destination. Its competitive advantage in this sector arises from strategic location, the transport and telecommunications infrastructure, human resources, and minimal regulations on the movement of goods, services and factors. Alongside commercial expertise, Singapore has skills in urban planning, air- and sea-port management, hotel management, engineering consultancy, and business support services. Government measures to promote the service industries include the upgrading of infrastructure, fiscal incentives, deregulation, privatisation, manpower development, and liberalising the inflow of foreign professionals. Singapore is a leading exporter of services amongst developing countries. Singapore has been the entrepot of Southeast Asia since the 19th century, providing the functions of trading, financing, transhipment, storage, grading and the processing and breaking of bulk.[7] The initial advantage of a strategic geographical location and a natural harbour was strengthened by a free port policy, the extension of efficient transport and telecommunications networks, and the availability of banking and commercial expertise. The entrepot function has survived and grown despite the rise of competing ports and airports and the active promotion of direct trading by neighbouring countries. Singapore is the 15th largest trading nation, its merchandise trade amounts to 1.7 per cent of global trade and it rivals Hong Kong as the world's busiest port. As air transport has expanded rapidly in the past decade, Singapore's Changi airport deals with some of the greatest numbers and volumes in Asia, and Singapore Airlines is a major international company. A spin-off from the trade, transport and telecommunications activities is the tourist industry. Despite limited natural, historical and cultural tourist attractions, the numbers visiting Singapore have reached nearly six million in 1992, more than double the resident population. Singapore is a major stop-over for travellers criss-crossing east to west and north to south, acts as a transit centre to various parts of Southeast Asia, and is increasingly important as a convention venue. Singapore emerged as a regional financial centre in the late 1960s by collecting off-shore funds for overseas lending and the assets of Asian Currency Units rose to US$355 billion by 1992.[8] The development strategy aims to establish Singapore as a risk management centre with active foreign exchange trading, money market operations, and trading in capital market instruments, equities and futures, and a wide variety of foreign financial institutions are located in Singapore. Firms are offered time zone advantages, efficient transport and telecommunications facilities, minimal financial regulations, attractive fiscal incentives, the ready availability of educated and trained manpower, and political, social and economic stability.

EXPLAINING SINGAPORE'S ECONOMIC SUCCESS

Singapore's advantages are to be discovered in its strategic geographical location, good governance, social cohesion, and human resources, but these must be balanced against the handicaps of small size and its economic and strategic vulnerability.

The Political and Social Framework

(i) Political Stability and Continuity

The PAP has governed Singapore since 1959. As the early generation leaders under Lee Kuan Yew aged, a new group was groomed to take over, and the smooth political transition of the 1980s has contributed to a stable investment environment. The style of PAP government is usually labelled as authoritarian and paternalistic, and its continuing dominance under a system of parliamentary democracy and in a city-state of sophisticated voters is attributable to its overcoming the threat of communism in the 1960s, surmounting economic vulnerability, and providing the electorate with political and social stability, housing, employment, and rising standards of living. Political continuity has allowed policy makers to take a long-term view of the economy and society, and implement measures deemed to be good for the economy and society, even though they were unpopular with certain segments of the electorate.[9]

(ii) Efficient and Clean Government

Good governance is particularly important for newly independent and developing nations, and the competence and honesty of the Singapore political leadership and bureaucracy are well known, and its lauded organisation and management of the economy. Meritocracy is practised in both politics and bureaucracy, and the PAP leaders who came into power in 1959 were regarded as among the brightest and ablest of their generation.[10] Increasingly, PAP candidates for parliamentary elections and ministerial appointments were selected on the basis of ability, and a stringent selection process has contributed to the quality of leadership, which has reinforced the people's traditional Confucian respect for authority. The best and ablest are similarly recruited into the civil service and statutory boards, and, to attract, motivate, and retain high-calibre personnel, public sector salaries are periodically reviewed to ensure comparability with the private sector. A performance bonus has also been incorporated into the civil service salary structure. When the established administration constrained the implementation of ambitious economic and social programmes in the 1960s, statutory boards and state-owned enterprises were created to allow for greater organisational autonomy and flexibility, although senior bureaucrats were represented to ensure effective control and facilitate coordination between government ministries and agencies. The PAP has been singularly successful in controlling corruption in politics and government. This situation may be credited to the attitudes of the political leadership, to the existence of an open economy with minimal and transparent rules and regulations, and to a well-paid and motivated bureaucracy. Singapore's economic success is largely due to the adoption and effective implementation of certain policies by politicians and bureaucrats. The government had no ideological baggage, eschewed economic nationalism, and preferred a pragmatic approach. Fiscal and monetary prudence contributed to price stability, high savings and investment rates, strong external reserves and currency, and low external indebtedness. Economic efficiency was emphasised in both the delivery of public goods and services and in the lack of protection and subsidies to private-sector activities. To overcome the constraints of Singapore's small size, both in factor endowments and markets, an international orientation was necessary with the importation of resources, goods and services in which Singapore had no comparative advantage being exchanged for the exportation of goods and services in which there was residual strength. Inflows of MNC investments and foreign skilled personnel augmented the limited domestic pool of enterprise, technology, organisation, and know-how.

(iii) Social Cohesion and Industrial Peace

Social cohesion has become a Singaporean trait, and the existence of consensus is central to the effective implementation of major policies and programmes and the creation of a stable environment which encourages investment. According to Porter, some nations enjoy a built-in national dedication to the objective of economic success, and nations that have faced difficulties or felt vulnerable evince this tendency.[11] Nation building began in Singapore as late as the 1960s, and the building of a social consensus has been policy priority. While economic efficiency has been emphasised, equity has been maintained and income gaps have not widened as a result of rapid economic development. A social safety net is provided by compulsory savings for old age, subsidised and high-quality public housing, public health and public education, and educational and job opportunities for all. Yet obtaining social cohesion in Singapore was more difficult than in other Asian NIEs because it is a multi-racial society, albeit with a large Chinese majority. Nation building entailed the delicate balancing and harmonising of conflicting interests of different groups. Multi-racialism is a keystone of public policy, and bilingualism, that is the learning of English and a mother tongue, has been a contributory factor.[12] English is a colonial heritage but it unifies the ethnic communities and is the language of international commerce, science and technology. The mother tongue policy enables each group to preserve its cultural heritage and accept the place of others.

The transformation of the industrial relations climate from one of trade union militancy and confrontation in the 1950s and early 1960s to one of industrial harmony was important to social cohesion and economic success. The government has overseen a far-reaching reorganisation of the trade union movement.[13] In the 1960s, some trade unions were de-registered, their pro-communist leaders were imprisoned, and remaining unions were placed under the aegis of the National Trades Union Congress (NTUC). The symbiotic relationship which was cultivated between the NTUC and the PAP government ensured that the new trade union movement supported national development goals and programmes. Labour legislation enacted in the 1960s provided for compulsory industrial arbitration, placed a lid on fringe benefits for workers, and restrained the power of trade unions to influence the management functions of staff recruitment, promotion, work assignment, retrenchment and dismissal. The objectives of trades unionism were redefined and redirected to promote workplace productivity and the process of industrialisation in the 1960s and 1970s and economic restructuring in the 1980s. Omnibus, multi-sector unions were reorganised into industry and house unions, and quality control circles (QCCs) and other productivity committees were formed at the workplace. Consensus building is evident in the growing practice of tripartism that links government, employers and unions. Cooperation between the three is best exemplified by the National Wages Council (NWC), formed in 1972 as a forum for negotiations on wage and labour issues.[14] Negotiations between employers and unions have been orderly and, although industrial strikes remain legal, there is a growing trust and goodwill. The attitude of unions was demonstrated during the 1985–86 recession, when, in support of a government call for restraint, they voluntarily agreed to wage stability and even cuts.

The Economic Framework

(i) Creation of Factor Resources

Porter has usefully reclassified the traditional factors of production into physical, human, capital and knowledge resources and infrastructure, distinguishing between inherited and created factors, lower order basic and high order advanced factors, and generalised and specialised factors.[15] Singapore's factor conditions, which enabled it to develop competitive advantages in several areas of manufacturing and services and to attract foreign direct investment, will be outlined. Essentially, they are a strategic geographical location, excellent infrastructure and developed human resources. Only its strategic location is an inherited factor. Through investments in physical and human capital, other factors have become of a higher order, providing for more sustainable competitive advantages. Singapore is severely handicapped by its small size and dearth of natural resources, including land and sea space; it has to import all its energy and most of its water requirements. A small geographical size is not without benefits, notably greater social cohesion and the absence of a backward rural sector. More importantly, the city-state enjoys a strategic geographical location with a good natural harbour; it is astride international air and sea routes, straddles the time zones of Asia and Europe, and is at the heart of the economically dynamic Asia-Pacific region. Location has helped determine Singapore's competitive advantage in several key industries and services, and it is being enhanced by investment in world class physical infrastructure. Land, sea, and air transportation, sea and airport facilities, telecommunications infrastructure and power supply provide the basic support system for industrialisation and the development of modern, high value-added services. An efficient domestic transportation network links the sea and airports and the financial and business districts. The industrial estates and science park offer development sites with wide-ranging facilities, allowing quick start-ups and external economies from the clustering of industries. Efficient, reliable and cost competitive telecommunications connect Singapore to the rest of the world, and, in information technology, Singapore has achieved world class status through a concerted effort involving the National Computer Board, educational institutions, training subsidies to schools and office workers, computerisation of the civil service, and the establishment of electronic networks. The city-state is also well served by foreign and local financial institutions which are linked to world financial markets.

Singapore has a very small population base, and government policy is aimed at improving the quantity and quality of human resources.[16] When the demographic transition slowed down the labour force growth rate, the workforce was augmented by the employment of females and foreigners. The availability of jobs for young women was a response to changing social conditions and improved educational and job opportunities, and was important to the attracting of foreign investment into the labour-intensive textiles, garments and electronics assembly industries during the late 1960s and 1970s. With full employment, skills bottlenecks, and local workers shunning certain occupations, a relaxation of immigration policy opened opportunities to foreign workers across the skills spectrum, and a large number of expatriate American, European and Asian personnel work for foreign MNCs. The government actively recruits educated and skilled foreigners to augment the small domestic talent pool, and, while the benefits are generally acknowledged, more controversial is the continuing heavy reliance on unassimilated foreign workers, both unskilled and semi-skilled. Measured by educational attainment, the quality of Singapore's population and workforce falls behind South Korea and Taiwan and the advanced industrial nations. In 1990, only 7.9 per cent of the non-student population had polytechnic or university qualifications, and 43.9 per cent had no more than primary education. Explanations of this poor profile are partly historical, the long-term influx of illiterate immigrants and the neglect of education under British colonial rule. In the 1960s, there were severe budgetary constraints and strong contending political, social and economic priorities. Education policy was forced to concentrate on the provision of universal primary education for the rapidly expanding cohorts of children reaching school-age; other immediate needs were bilingual education as a foundation of social cohesion, and technical and vocational training to supply emerging manpower needs. In the late 1970s, once budgetary resources had improved and universal primary education had been achieved, funds were directed towards secondary and tertiary education. Only in the mid-1980s did the expansion of tertiary education receive high priority, and enrolment in polytechnics and universities almost doubled between 1984 and 1992, with science, engineering, business and computer courses proving especially attractive.

Why did Singapore's limited educated manpower not handicap economic performance in the 1960s and 1970s? First, the labour-intensive phase of industrialisation did not make heavy demands on skills. Second, foreign skilled and professional manpower offset domestic shortages. Third, although lacking in formal education qualifications, the workforce was hardworking and adaptable, and picked up the necessary skills through pre-employment and in-employment training. There has been a rapid expansion of vocational, technical, industrial and computer training under the Vocational and Industrial Training Board, later changed to the Institute of Technical Education, the Economic Development Board (EDB) and the National Computer Board (NCB). An innovative feature of the EDB's training schemes is their reliance on collaboration with overseas governments, foreign MNCs and specialised manufacturers which have technological or market leadership, or, alternatively, an excellent training record. Such a partnership exposes trainees to different training systems and to a simulated factory environment which makes effective use of experience and expertise and it provides up-to-date curricula and facilities. In information technology, the training of professionals and technicians is undertaken by tertiary educational institutions and institutes in collaboration with leading foreign MNCs. The number of IT professionals reached 8,000 in 1988 and has been growing by approximately 1,000 every year. Excepting the 1960s, Singapore did not suffer from severe capital constraints, since both public and private savings rose rapidly. Savings rates, at negative levels in the early 1960s grew to 46.8 per cent of GNP by 1992. Investment rates rose from less than 15 per cent in the early 1960s to over 47 per cent in 1980–84, before sliding below 40 per cent in later years. Since 1986, Singapore has become a net exporter of capital. High private savings are explained by income growth, low dependency ratios, the availability of financial institutions, a postal savings scheme, stringent prudential regulations, and positive real interest rates. Public savings are the result of budgetary surpluses, a cautious fiscal policy, and profits from well-managed statutory boards and state enterprises. Positive balances have been achieved despite heavy investments in infrastructure and a general lowering of corporate and personal income tax rates. High investment rates are both a requirement and a result of rapid economic growth, and are increasingly stimulated by the private sector, whose share of the total increased from around 65 per cent in 1960–68 to over 80 per cent in 1989–92. Singapore's economic growth has been achieved largely through increased capital and labour inputs and imported technology. Its small size and heavy dependence on foreign MNCs for technology and markets have contributed to low domestic technological capability. Efforts to encourage research and development (R&D) activities by MNCs in Singapore have met with limited success, as international companies generally prefer to concentrate R&D in their home base or in countries with a strong R&D infrastructure. Consequently, Singapore lags behind South Korea and Taiwan in this area: R&D expenditures reached US$352 million or one per cent of GNP in 1990, and the number of research scientists and engineers (RSE) reached 4,276 or 28 per 10,000 of the labour force. Even ignoring absolute differences, South Korea's ratios were 1.8 per cent and 33 per 10,000 in 1989, while Taiwan's ratios were 1.3 per cent and 43 per 10,000 in 1988. Singapore's size constraint means that R&D resources are more limited and efforts have to be targeted. The National Technology Plan (1991) seeks to develop R&D expenditure until it reaches two per cent of GDP in 1995, with at least half coming from the private sector; an RSE ratio of 40 per 10,000 has been set.[17] Following consultations with industry, nine key technology development areas have been identified: information technology, microelectronics, electronic systems, manufacturing technology, materials technology, energy, the water environment and resources, biotechnology, food and agrotechnology, and medical science. A S$2 billion (US$1.2 billion) fund to support industry-driven R&D over a five-year period, grants and fiscal incentives, material backing for research centres and institutes, and assistance for the commercial exploitation of projects have all been planned.

(ii) Demand Conditions and Industrial Linkages

Porter stresses the importance of domestic demand in determining a nation's competitive advantage.[18] Singapore's extremely limited home market means that its industries and firms do not have economies of scale unless they compete internationally. Data from 1988 shows that exports accounted for about half of aggregate production, ranging from 93.2 per cent for petroleum refining and 71.3 per cent for manufacturing to 58.8 per cent for transport and communications, 33.5 per cent for commerce, and 12.1 per cent for financial and business services.[19] This reliance on export demand pressurises firms to be competitive, and success depends on cost efficiencies, the anticipation of market needs, design, quality, service, and an ability to surmount trade barriers. The lack of a home market does not allow consumers to absorb learning costs, and Singapore is vulnerable to the vagaries of external demand and the uncertainties of international competition. It relies on foreign MNCs to secure export markets. Porter also emphasises how national advantage is improved by the presence of internationally competitive supplier and related industries.[20] Singapore's manufacturing is reliant on imports: total direct and indirect inputs from overseas amounted in 1988 to 90.1 per cent for petroleum refining and 60.8 per cent for manufacturing but they are lower in services. The absence of import restrictions and local content requirements, coupled with the efficient transport and communications network, enable foreign MNCs and local enterprises to obtain their needs from abroad. But the low backward linkages, because of high imported inputs, and the low forward linkages, because of the high export orientation, have prevented Singapore enterprises benefiting from vertical integration and limited the scope for industrial clustering.[21]

(iii) Foreign Direct Investment

Except for the early years, inward foreign direct investment has been actively promoted more for their production, management and marketing expertise than for their financial resources. The role of FDI in the Singapore economy has been far-reaching, more so than in other Asian NIEs. Foreign MNCs have facilitated the quick transition from import substitution to the export orientation of the manufacturing sector and assisted the development of Singapore as a regional financial centre. Up to 1990, Singapore was the largest recipient of FDI amongst Asian developing countries, and cumulative direct inward investment reached US$31.5 billion in 1990 (Table 2), with 59.7 per cent of this sum going to services

TABLE 2
INWARD CUMULATIVE FOREIGN DIRECT INVESTMENT BY SECTOR, 1980-90

	1980	1990
Agriculture, fishing, mining & quarrying	0.2	0.1
Manufacturing	53.3	39.1
Construction	1.3	1.1
Commerce	16.8	13.0
Transport & storage	3.4	3.3
Finance & business services	24.7	42.8
Social & personal services	0.3	2.7
Total	100.0	100.0
S$billion	13.0	57.9

Source: Department of Statistics, *Yearbook of Statistics, Singapore 1992* (Singapore, 1993).

and 39.1 percent to manufacturing. The main foreign investors are the European Community (22.9 per cent), followed by Japan (19.4 per cent) and the US (17.2 per cent). The bulk of the FDI in services went into financial and business services (42.8 per cent), and, in the manufacturing sector, such investment is concentrated in electronics, petroleum refining, electrical machinery and industrial chemicals. The foreign equity share exceeded 90 per cent in petroleum refining and electronics, and the overwhelming role of FDI in industry is evident from Table 3. In 1991, wholly foreign-owned firms alone accounted for 62.1 per cent of manufacturing output, 64 per cent of value added, 48.6 per cent of employment and 73.6 per cent of direct exports; including joint ventures enlarges the shares. Wholly local-owned firms were responsible for only 16.1 per cent of output, 17.4 per cent of value added, 30.5 per cent of employment and 8.5 per cent of direct exports. The export-total sales ratios were a high 72.7 per cent for wholly foreign-owned firms, 50.7 per cent for joint ventures, and 32.6 per cent for wholly local-owned firms.

Singapore's success in attracting FDI, notwithstanding the lack of natural resources and markets, is due to a carefully coordinated and an all-embracing investment policy that offers political stability, industrial peace, sophisticated infrastructure, trained and disciplined manpower, supportive

TABLE 3

FOREIGN INVESTMENT IN THE MANUFACTURING SECTOR, 1975-91

	Gross output	Value added	Employment	Direct exports	Export ratio*
1975 % share of:					
Wholly foreign-owned	56.2	47.4	31.5	66.1	67.6
More than half foreign	15.1	15.3	20.5	18.0	69.8
Less than half foreign	10.7	13.0	15.1	7.0	40.6
Wholly local-owned	18.0	24.3	32.8	8.9	28.3
Total	100.0	100.0	100.0	100.0	58.1
1985 % share of:					
Wholly foreign-owned	54.5	54.9	41.6	65.7	76.6
More than half foreign	15.9	9.9	11.8	16.5	65.3
Less than half foreign	9.3	11.8	13.1	6.4	44.0
Wholly local-owned	20.3	23.4	33.5	11.4	35.1
Total	100.0	100.0	100.0	100.0	63.2
1991 % share of:					
Wholly foreign-owned	62.1	64.0	48.6	73.6	72.7
More than half foreign	13.1	8.2	9.5	11.6	54.1
Less than half foreign	8.7	10.3	11.4	6.3	45.4
Wholly local-owned	16.1	17.4	30.5	8.5	32.6
Total	100.0	100.0	100.0	100.0	61.5

Source: Economic Development Board, *Report on the Census of Industrial Production*, various years (Singapore)
*Export-total sales ratio.

and efficient governance, low taxes, minimal regulations, attractive fiscal incentives, and a pleasant and safe living environment. The Singapore–MNC partnership is perceived to be of mutual benefit, and trust and goodwill have grown with time. The chief executives of leading MNCs frequently serve on various policy-making and advisory committees, while Singaporeans are increasingly appointed to top management positions within MNC subsidiaries located in Singapore and Southeast Asia. There are more than 3,000 foreign multinationals in Singapore, including more than 650 manufacturing plants. In the early years, the EDB promoted Singapore as a production base, but labour shortages and rising wage and other operating costs later compelled the relocation of labour-intensive operations. MNCs are encouraged to transfer to neighbouring countries while retaining higher business functions in Singapore. The country enjoys an early-starter advantage and many MNCs have preferred to retain as much of their investments as possible rather than uprooting completely to less certain political, social and policy environments. Multinational operations in Singapore have been upgraded and expanded to combine a number of activities, including the manufacture of high-end finished products and components, engineering support, product R&D, international procurement, and marketing and distribution. These activities are shifting from regional to global manufacturing, from assembly and testing to the front-end integration of design and development, from regional marketing and technical support to component production for global manufacturing and regional management. Some MNCs are locating world-class manufacturing and processing plants in Singapore in fulfilment of their globalisation strategies. The EDB has actively pushed the city-state as a product development and design centre, as a base for distribution and procurement, and as a location for regional operational headquarters.[22]

(iv) Local Enterprises

In 1990, there were about 80,000 local enterprises in manufacturing, commerce, transport and storage, and the financial and business services, contributing about half of the value added in these four sectors. The largest are to be found in traditional sectors such as food and beverages, banking and property development, while some large government-linked companies are in ship-repairing, transport and communications, and high technology defence-related activities. Most local enterprises are small and serve the domestic market, and have a limited role in manufactured exports. This weakness, particularly after three decades of industrialisation, and in comparison with other Asian NIEs, needs explanation. Several factors are involved, and foremost is the small and unprotected domestic market, with few opportunites for economies of scale. Access to neighbouring countries was restricted when Malaysia and Indonesia adopted import-substitution policies. Development of other markets takes time, knowledge and finance and, until the mid-1980s, the government was not forthcoming with financial, technical and market development support. Foreign MNCs and state enterprises had larger and better resources, and many foreign companies had the additional advantage of brand names. They attracted the most talented with attractive salaries and career paths. Risk capital was limited, because commercial banks were reluctant to lend without the backing of collateral or a proven track record. Merchant banking was in its infancy, the stock market had stringent listing requirements, and strict prudential regulations brought the disappearance of an informal credit market. Local small and medium enterprises were faced with rising business costs when urban redevelopment enforced relocation in premises carrying higher rentals. The entrepreneurial spirit appears to have been weakened by an educational system which emphasised examinations rather than creativity and innovation; an approach to public service recruitment which placed a premium on scholastic results; the ready availability of attractive jobs in the public service and MNCs; and the uncertainties of small-scale business and self-employment. Singapore has developed into a mandarin state where administrators are more honoured than its entrepreneurial class.

Interest in small-scale industry has heightened since the 1985–86 recession, and, under the EDB's SME Master Plan, unveiled in 1989, local enterprises are depicted as the source of innovation, providing supportive links for foreign MNCs, specialty manufactures and services for the global market, channels for the transfer of technology and know-how, and potential world-class enterprises.[23] There are currently over 60 programmes to promote the growth of local enterprises at each stage of their development, covering technology acquisition, business development, human resource management, marketing, design, research and development, computerisation and productivity improvement. The political and social climate for local enterprises is fast changing. There are annual awards for the most successful local entrepreneurs, political leaders frequently highlight and laud the achievements of individuals, and the media is giving them wider coverage. Those domestic businesses that are upgrading and expanding at home and regionally include companies in fashionware, retailing, manufacturing, engineering, computers and software, consultancy and professional services. More family-owned firms are professionalising their management and operations and seeking listing on the stock exchange, and several now count as regional or multinational concerns.

NEW DIRECTIONS

The Strategic Economic Plan (SEP) published in 1991 outlined the strategy which Singapore would adopt to achieve the status of an advanced developed nation in two to three decades. Given Singapore's small size and resource and market constraints, the document calls for the expansion of Singapore's SME sector and the extension of Singapore's economic borders through internationalisation; it is looking to the world and the Asia-Pacific region for markets, technology, and resources. In the past, Singapore had drawn in foreign MNCs to produce, export and create employment. With the limits to growth posed by land and labour, internationalisation means outward investment and partnerships and strategic alliances with foreign countries and companies. The SEP recognises how the nature of competition has changed through developments in domestic factor conditions and the rise of countries with lower cost structures and rapidly developing capabilities. Singapore has to change the nature of its international competitiveness and accrue more advanced and sustaining capabilities, and resources are to be targeted on improved resources, core capabilities, and local enterprises. In the 1990s, a more productive and internationally oriented workforce is being trained, through formal pre-employment and on- and off-the-job education and training, and the nurturing of teamwork, the work ethic, and creativity. Skilled and talented foreigners, as a result, are coming to Singapore. As core capabilities can be boosted through clusters of independent industries linked by markets and products, the SEP has identified particular industry groups, namely commodity trading, shipping, precision engineering, electronics, information technology, petroleum and petrochemicals, construction, heavy engineering, finance, insurance, general supporting industries, and tourism. Lead government agencies have been told to develop their core capabilities, and a S$1 billion (US$0.6 billion) Cluster Development Fund has been created. The money will be used to attract high technology companies, and the Fund will act as a risk- and cost-sharing partner, while investing in local enterprises and assisting MNCs engaged in regional projects.

To enhance Singapore's overall competitiveness, various government agencies such as the Economic Development Board, the Trade Development Board and the National Computer Board seek to achieve a more dynamic and indigenous business sector. Outward investment is being used to overcome the domestic constraints of limited resources and markets, and to exploit the new opportunities available from the rapidly growing and liberalising economies of the Asia-Pacific region. By 1990, some 2,300 Singapore-based companies (including foreign MNCs) had direct invest-ments abroad worth an aggregate S$7.5 billion (US$4.1 billion), mostly in Asia. At the same time, some 15,000 Singapore residents or about one per cent of the workforce were working abroad, slightly over half in Asia, and mainly in Malaysia and China. To help the internationalisation of companies, the government is reviewing the policy framework, including taxation, with the aim of removing impediments, and it is negotiating bilateral investment agreements. Local firms venturing abroad will be able to utilise the resources and expertise of state agencies and government-linked companies.[24] Many Singaporean enterprises have achieved a regional dimension in 1992–93, as the opening up of China, Indo-China, India and ASEAN are providing new investment and business opportunities in geographically proximate and culturally and linguistically familiar locations.

NOTES

1. World Bank, *The East Asian Miracle: Economic Growth and Public Policy* (Washington DC: Oxford University Press, 1993).
2. Michael Porter, *The Competitive Advantage of Nations* (New York: The Free Press, 1990).
3. Economic Planning Committee, Ministry of Trade and Industry, Singapore, *The Strategic Economic Plan: Towards a Developed Nation* (Singapore: Ministry of Trade and Industry, 1991).
4. See, Chia Siow Yue, 'The Character and Progress of Industrialisation', in Kernial Singh Sandhu and Paul Wheatley (eds.), *Management of Success: The Moulding of Modern Singapore*, (Singapore: Institute of Southeast Asian Studies, 1989), pp.250–79, for a discussion of the industrialisation process.
5. Economic Development Board, *Yearbook* and *Investment News*, various issues.
6. Ibid.
7. For a discussion of the historical entrepot role, see Edwin Lee, 'The Colonial Legacy',

in Sandhu and Wheatley, op. cit. pp.8–12.
8. See, Ralph Bryant, 'The Evolution of Singapore as a Financial Centre', in Sandhu and Wheatley, op. cit., pp.337–72. For more up-to-date information on the growth and deepening of the financial centre, see the annual reports of the Monetary Authority of Singapore.
9. For a discussion of Singapore's political leadership and political system, see Robert Tilman, 'The Political Leadership: Lee Kuan Yew and the PAP Team', and Chan Heng Chee, 'The PAP and the Structuring of the Political System', both in Sandhu and Wheatley, op.cit., pp.53–69 and pp.70–89.
10. For a discussion of the Singapore bureaucracy, see Lee Boon Hiok, 'The Bureaucracy', in Sandhu and Wheatley, op.cit., pp.90–101.
11. Porter, op. cit., p.681.
12. For a discussion of Singapore's language policies, see Nirmala Puru Shotam, 'Language and Linguistic Policies', in Sandhu and Wheatley, op. cit., pp.503–22.
13. See, Raj Vasil, 'Trade Unions', in Sandhu and Wheatley, op. cit. pp.144–70.
14. For a discussion of the role of the National Wages Council, see the chapter on 'Wage Policy', in Lim Chong Yah and Associates, *Policy Options for the Singapore Economy* (Singapore: McGraw Hill, 1988), pp.203–8.
15. Porter, op. cit., pp.74–81.
16. See, Pang Eng Fong, Tan Chwee Huat and Cheng Soo May, 'The Management of People', in Sandhu and Wheatley, op. cit., pp.128–43.
17. National Science and Technology Board, *Window of Opportunities: National Technology Plan 1991* (Singapore: SNS Publishers, 1991).
18. Porter, op. cit., p.86–99.
19. Department of Statistics, Singapore, *Singapore Input-Output Tables 1988* (Singapore, 1992).
20. Porter, op. cit., pp.100–07.
21. SME Committee, *SME Master Plan: Report on Enterprise Development* (Singapore: Economic Development Board, 1989).
22. Economic Planning Committee, Ministry of Trade and Industry *The Strategic Economic Plan: Towards a Developed Nation.* (Singapore: Ministry of Trade and Industry, 1991).
23. Department of Statistics, *Singapore's Investment Abroad 1990* (Singapore: Namic Printers, 1992).
24. Committee to Promote Enterprise Overseas, *Interim Report* and *Final Report* (Singapore: Ministry of Finance, 1993).

Competitive Advantage in the Context of Hong Kong

S.G. REDDING

PORTER AND 'ANGLO-SAXON' PERSPECTIVES

A recent review of the literature on comparative management[1] identified the work of Porter[2] as being worthy of emulation because of its attempt to bridge disciplines. Starting from an economics perspective, it ventures into business policy, marketing, political economy, economic geography and general management, and successfully integrates a great deal of otherwise disparate knowledge. Laudable and necessary though such theorising is, there are nevertheless limits to the elasticity of a theory so firmly rooted in the tightest of the social science paradigms, that of economics. It is perhaps salutary to consider the epistemological problem which is entailed in extending theory beyond the highly developed economies and into arenas where alternative frameworks of meaning may call for some loosening of the assumption that universal laws exist for economic action. Such questioning is given support by the increasing realisation that business systems exist discretely from each other, and contain internal dynamics which, due to cultural and historical determinants, require separate understanding, each in its own right.[3] It is for instance possible to delineate several distinct forms of capitalism, each with a character of its own, such character being a product of fundamental differences in a society's handling of trust, authority and identity, in its industrialisation experience, and in the evolution of attitudes over access to capital and to skills. Distinct types of firm tend to emerge, such as the Korean chaebol, the Japanese keiretsu, and the Chinese family business, and they display distinct postures in their strategic behaviour, homogeneous within the type, but different between types. It is not at all certain that a paradigm based on Anglo-Saxon economics can be universally applicable across such variety, and this paper will explore the competitive success of Hong Kong as a test of the model's utility in explaining the transition from a developing to a developed economy. A critique by Yetton[4] points to ethnocentrism in Porter's model and argues that it is 'a theory for refocusing American or European firms on the essentials of global manufacturing in or near large markets, given that many of the ingredients of the diamond are already in place for them'[5] (see Introduction, on Porter's 'diamond'). They conclude that Porter has not articulated a

---

S.G. Redding, University of Hong Kong Business School

theory of national competitive advantage, but rather of firms and industries within nations; that valid proof of the theory is weak; and that the theory is incomplete, leaving out the emergence of successful new firms, and firms in non-traded sectors and resources. They acknowledge Porter's success in drawing attention to previously underemphasised aspects of competitiveness but point out that this is not the same as producing a valid universal model.

INDUSTRY IN HONG KONG

Hong Kong began its existence as a colonial trading outpost and grew into a significant entrepot for trade in and out of China, until the Second World War and the subsequent defeat of the Kuomintang by Communist forces led to the effective sealing off of China from world trade and commerce. Three forces conspired during the 1950s to turn Hong Kong into a manufacturing-based economy. Firstly, the Korean War created high demand for certain manufactured goods. Secondly, an influx of industrialists from Shanghai brought material and technical skills of a high order, particularly in textiles and garment-making. Thirdly, a huge influx of refugees created a large pool of low-cost trainable labour. The Chinese flair for entrepreneurship and the existence of a sound infrastructure of commercial law, economic services, and banking were already in place, and have been refined and enlarged constantly since. The result over the subsequent decade is clear: the national performance in per capita GDP growth terms is second only to Singapore in world terms, outstripping the successes of Japan, Korea and Taiwan and growing at double the speed of typically successful Western countries. This success has been built in the main on small-scale manufacturing, and has displayed successive waves of adjustment as respectively textiles, clothing, plastics, and electronics vied for the leading position. By the mid-1980s, the leading industries were toys, garments and electronics, but, by this time, a major change to Hong Kong's industrial structure was beginning.

In 1984, the British and Chinese governments signed the Joint Declaration which would see Hong Kong returned to China in 1997, but in conditions where for 50 years thereafter its *modus operandi* would remain basically unchanged. Its capitalist free market economy and supporting administrative and service infrastructure are guaranteed under an internationally open treaty registered with the United Nations. From the mid-1980s on, industrialists began to see the Hong Kong and Chinese economies as joined and in effect Hong Kong industry began to move into China, and particularly into the adjacent province of Guangdong. Earlier successful experimentation with the Shenzhen special economic zone had demonstrated the feasibility of making use of low-cost land and labour over the border. In more recent years the magnetism of those advantages has sucked in much Hong Kong manufacturing activity, expanding it greatly in the process, and leaving Hong Kong itself increasingly to provide trading and support services. It is interesting that, of the two leading industries, electronics and garments, the former has moved into China much more obviously than the latter, and this phenomenon will form the centrepiece for our analysis of the Porter framework in the context of Hong Kong. Before considering those industries in detail, it is necessary to be more specific about the surrounding circumstances, and in particular, three issues: turbulence, internationalisation, and changing industrial structure.

The first significant fact about industry in Hong Kong is its volatility, and the fact that average GDP growth rates over time conceal a switchback ride of almost violent turbulence. This is illustrated in Figure 1 for the 30 years 1962–92, and demonstrates the sensitivity of a small economy in which home demand is almost irrelevant and external factors have seemingly magnified effects. The flexibility of an economy based on a dense network of interlocked small enterprises is well demonstrated in the capacity to survive such swings in demand.[6] The internationalisation

FIGURE 1
A RESILIENT HONG KONG ECONOMY

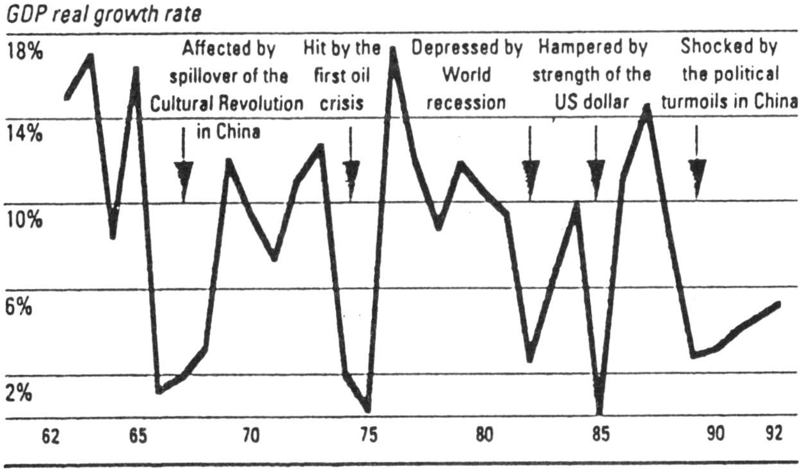

Source: Booz-Allen & Hamilton analysis, Government statistics.

of the Hong Kong economy followed during the 1980s from two causes. In the early part of that period, many firms began to invest abroad, and particularly in Pacific Asia as a hedge against a possibly hostile takeover by China. The movement of capital was paralleled by a movement of the bourgeoisie for the security of alternative passports. At the same time, a second force was the emergence of a labour shortage in Hong Kong and the need to look elsewhere for low-cost labour. The average daily money wage in manufacturing more than doubled from HK$73 in 1982 to HK$184 in 1990, and the average real wage in 1982 prices increased from 73 to 101. Over the same period in China, the national average daily wage was moving from HK$10 to 11.6, although that for the adjacent Guangdong province went from 11.6 to 15.[7] Similar large wage cost advantages were utilised in Indonesia and Thailand, with more risk in the Philippines and Vietnam, and further afield in Sri Lanka, some African countries, and South or Central America. Other forms of internationalising were evident, unrelated to the pursuit of low-cost labour, as heavy capital investment in banking, property, hotels and telecommunications proceeded to expand Hong Kong's economy into a wide range of other countries. An equally relevant aspect of the process of internationalisation has been the reverse flow of multinationals attracted to Hong Kong as a regional headquarters, and the numbers in this case grew from 174 in 1980 to 602 in 1991.[8] The resulting effects in investment flows of the internationalising process are visible in the increasing economic connection both ways with China, as well as the increasing use by Japan of Hong Kong as a staging post.

The third background factor, that of changing industrial structure, stems mainly from the move of manufacturing into China and elsewhere (with the interesting exception of much of the garment industry), and the parallel growth in Hong Kong of the services sector. The movement of industry over the short span of 1988–91 is illustrated in Figure 2, and longer term structural change is illustrated in Figure 3. The ratio of manufacturing to services employment has changed from 1.1 to 0.35 between 1981 and 1991, and the ratio of re-exports (largely ex-China) to domestic exports has moved from 0.5 to over 2. The move into China was particularly dramatic in electronics, electricals, fur and footwear.

GARMENTS AND ELECTRONICS INDUSTRIES COMPARED

A recent study of Hong Kong's two leading manufacturing industries, garments and electronics, reveals interesting differences in their modes of adjustment to the forces affecting the economy since 1980.[9] The core strategy in each industry has been to rely on labour-intensive production and to serve niche markets with constant rapid adjustments in production. In the case of electronics, this has meant serving niches such as fax machines, video games, talking toys and other applications of specific integrated circuits, rather than entering mass-market standardised microchip production. In the case of garments, concentration has moved to short production runs of high-quality fashion clothing subcontracted by international branded fashion houses. In both cases, buying agencies with a related network of small, often linked, manufacturers have played a key role. This international network of commercial sub-contracting and OEM

COMPETITIVE ADVANTAGE IN HONG KONG

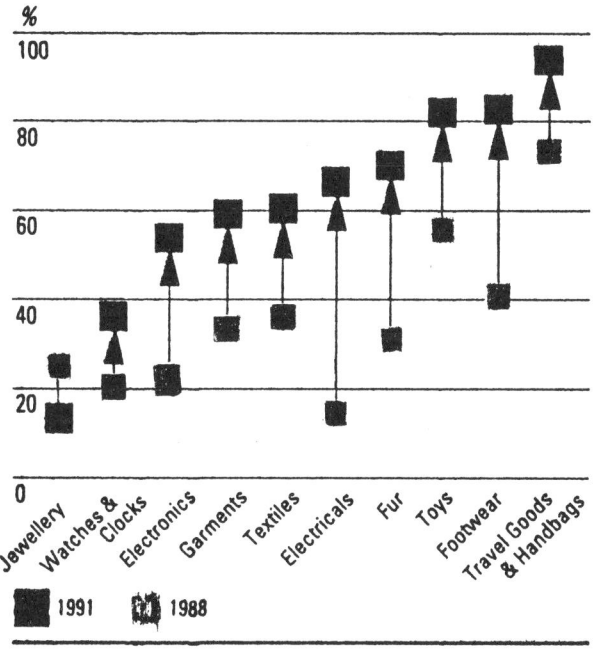

FIGURE 2
HONG KONG EXPORTS MADE IN CHINA 1988–1991

Source: Booz-Allen & Hamilton analysis, HKTDC.

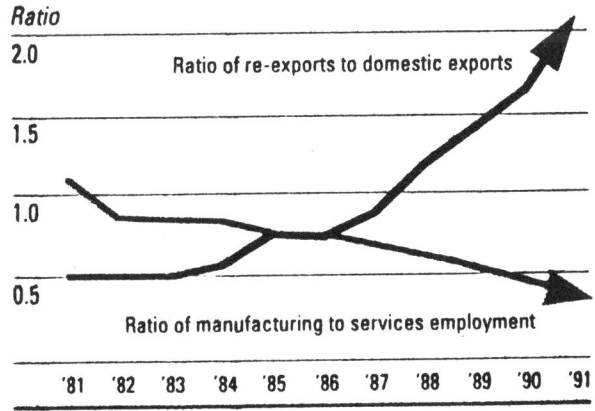

FIGURE 3
DRAMATIC STRUCTURAL CHANGE IN HONG KONG

Source: Booz-Allen & Hamilton analysis, Government statistics.

manufacturing contrasts sharply with the Singapore pattern of production via direct foreign investment. The main characteristics of the two industries are given in Table 1, based on a survey of 20 per cent of all establishments randomly selected, and a 70 per cent response rate. The dominance of local ownership and owner management is clear and suggestive of relatively low levels of capital investment. The two industries vary mainly in the source of orders, with direct overseas buying by principals being more common in electronics. Direct marketing via the company's own channels overseas is of small importance, and negligible for garments. Given such seemingly simple organisational forms, it is salutary to note that in recent years Hong Kong has been exporting more clothing than any other country

TABLE 1

THE STRUCTURE OF OWNERSHIP AND SOURCES OF ORDER OF THE GARMENT-MAKING AND ELECTRONICS INDUSTRIES

Characteristics	Electronics	Garment
Locally Owned	82.0%	94.2%
Owner Managed	74.0%	92.8%
Production for Export: 50% or more	62.0%	57.8%
Order from Overseas Directly: 50% or more	42.0%	10.4%
Order from Local Import and Export Houses: 50% or more	28.0%	47.9%
Order from Local Factories: 50% or more	24.0%	23.3%
Order from Own Overseas Outlets	8.0%	2.8%

Source: Chiu and Lui, 1993

in the world. The alternative strategies adopted in the electronics and garment industries are summarised in Table 2.[10] From this, it is clear that in the garment industry 78 per cent of firms retain a factory in Hong Kong and only 30 per cent have overseas production, whereas with electronics, although 62 per cent retain a Hong Kong factory, 52 per cent produce overseas. Other significant differences occur in subcontracting and technology. The use of various forms of subcontracting is extensive in garments but only minor in electronics. New technology and R&D occur widely in electronics, but are largely absent in garments.

TABLE 2

PRODUCTION STRATEGIES OF GARMENT-MAKING AND ELECTRONICS ESTABLISHMENTS

Production Strategy\Industry	Garment (N = 69)	Electronics (N = 50)
Organisation of Production		
Capacity Subcontracting	46.4%	22.0%
Outwork	47.8%	10.0%
Internal Contracting	43.5%	0.0%
Employment of Flexible Workforce		
Temporary Worker	40.6%	26.0%
Foreign Worker	2.9%	2.0%
Part-time Worker	17.4%	22.0%
Other Human Resources Strategies		
Employee Retention Strategy	38.8%	56.0%
Training Program	29.9%	38.0%
'Hope to Use Foreign Workers?'	32.3%	23.6%
Technological Development		
New Technology	21.7%	48.0%
R & D Activities	4.3%	46.0%
Relocation		
Overseas Production	30.4%	52.0%
'Still Running Own Factory Production in Hong Kong'	78.3%	62.0%

Source: Chiu and Lui, 1993

The overwhelming impression is that the garment industry has adopted a strategy of reliance on the transaction cost efficiency of the dense and highly developed subcontracting network, plus the attraction to buyers of a very high speed of response to changes in demand. This strategic choice has been reinforced by two powerful external forces. The Hong Kong government's policing of country-of-origin rules has been rigorous and has prevented the simple re-labelling of goods made in China, requiring instead that a made-in-Hong Kong label reflects some processing there. Furthermore, the information technology revolution in retailing has increased the relevance of highly responsive sources of supply able to deliver styles, colours and sizes in relatively small batches over wide ranges of garments at short notice. In this industry, where hand-finishing and expert inspection have facilitated constant upward movements in garment quality, the resort to sophisticated production technology has been resisted. While improvements in basic manufacturing machinery have naturally been incorporated, they have not altered the small-batch nature of the majority of production, and this form is resistant to integrated and automated systems of production. By contrast, in the electronics industry, both small firms and large firms have been more clearly committed to relocating in low-cost labour areas abroad, especially in Guangdong. Thirty-eight per cent of the surveyed firms have no production in Hong Kong and 52 per cent now manufacture abroad. The tendency is to convert the Hong Kong operation into an R&D section and to send the labour-intensive production to China where manual component assembly makes the industry competitive without the cost of full-scale automation.[11] R&D remains limited to production modification rather than core technology or design and most manufacturing is OEM. Technological upgrading has consequently been quite limited. Many firms have also converted their Hong Kong emphasis to trading, using their supply and subcontracting network to effect forward integration. The range of such ancillary services now incorporated in companies as a result of the expansion of the services function in the economy as a whole is indicated in Figure 4.

Chiu and Lui conclude that, in order to remain competitive, these two industries have in recent years adopted divergent strategies. Electronics, apparently less affected by country-of-origin issues, and able to use longer production runs, has resisted capital investment in technological upgrading and moved to take advantage of low-cost labour for largely manual assembly. The garment industry, constrained by both country-of-origin concerns and buyer demands for extreme flexibility, has been unable to make savings from low-cost labour across the border. It might be seen to be in a position of increasing vulnerability, as its labour costs fall victim to labour cost inflation in Hong Kong. These industries, highly competitive in world terms, will now be considered in the light of the explanatory model proposed by Porter.

APPLYING THE PORTER MODEL

There are two explanatory problems which Porter is addressing in his work on strategy theory. The first is what he terms the *cross-sectional problem* and this deals with the causes of superior performance at a given time. This is largely addressed by his theory of competitive advantage and the analysis of the determinants of firm success in the context of an industry. Certain forces in an industry drive inter-firm rivalry, and the

FIGURE 4
COMMERCIAL ACTIVITIES UNDERTAKEN IN HONG KONG

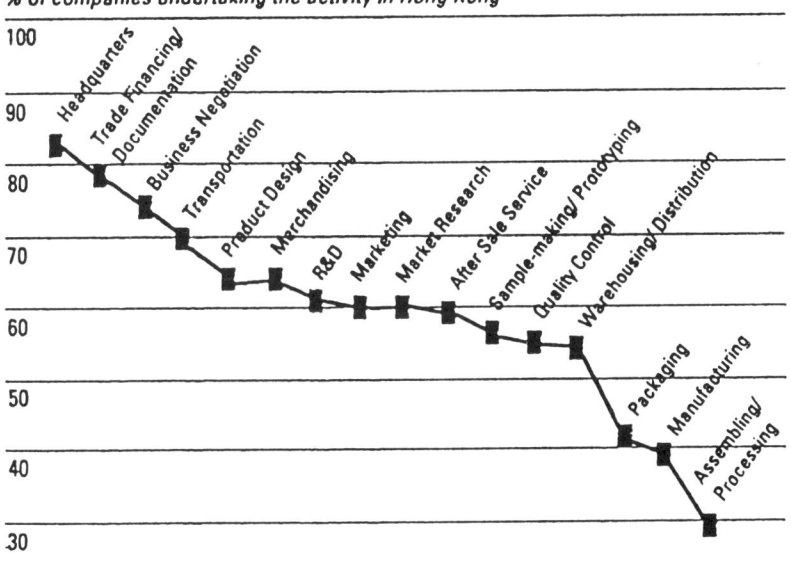

Source: Booz-Allen & Hamilton analysis, HKTDC 1991 survey (2,895 HK companies), Government statistics.

construction of an efficient value chain will allow competitive advantage.[12] The main unit of analysis here is the firm. There is, however, a different problem addressed in later work,[13] and this is what he terms the *longitudinal problem*. This concerns the dynamic process whereby competitive positions are created and takes into account as a major input the local environment in which a firm is based. The cross-sectional problem, which he sees as logically prior, is better understood than the longitudinal.[14] The unit of analysis in the latter is an industry or industry segment. The longitudinal problem must in Porter's view address four important issues:[15]

1. A theory must deal simultaneously with both the firm itself as well as the industry and broader environment in which it operates.
2. The theory must allow for exogenous change in areas such as buyer needs, technology and input markets, and thus avoid seeing strategy as a once-and-for-all game.
3. The theory must present firms with options to create new choices as well as advice on choosing amongst an initial set.
4. Historical accident and chance cannot be ruled out.

If a logical premise is that the base requirement is a flexible, learning organisation able continually to redefine its strategy, an empirical problem then arises if most successful organisations improve but do not change strategy very often. If making good choices and implementing them well are the keys, the problem still remains of why some firms do this better than others. It is here that environmental forces are argued to come into play as they condition firms to choose correctly and implement well. Porter's diamond is his attempt to define the four environmental features which influence most a firm's constant progression. Applying the diamond model to two of Hong Kong's most successful industries as they begin to diverge in strategy implementation may provide insights as to its completeness. The nature of the causation within Porter's theory is as follows. There are four determinants of national competitive advantage in an industry segment: firm strategy, structure and rivalry; factor conditions; demand conditions; and related and supporting industries. These attributes of a business environment cause firm competitiveness by the following processes:

1. Shaping the information firms have about opportunities.
2. Shaping the pool of inputs, skills and knowledge available.
3. Influencing the goals which condition investment.
4. Exerting on firms a degree of pressure to act.

Firm Strategy, Structure, and Rivalry

The structure of Hong Kong's most successful industries is one of networked small and medium enterprises. That this response is instinctive in the forms of business adopted by the Chinese overseas is suggested by a parallel pattern in Taiwan where export success is also associated with small and medium-sized firms.[16] An important feature which provides insight into such structures is the use of network alliances which permit a firm to transcend the limitations of its own small scale.[17] Such alliances are flexible and any particular firm is likely to have several in order to reduce dependence. Their purpose is to supply inputs, such as the specialised manufacture of collars for garments, or service inputs such as fabric dyeing. For a firm in the middle of a network, allied firms might provide services nearer the end-user such as packaging, or shipping and forwarding. The efficiency of the system as a whole rests heavily on trust-bonding and thus on an eventually Confucian value system in the society, which serves to reduce transaction costs.[18]

The strategies of such firms are based on speed and flexibility of response, the cultivation of reliable relationships to sustain cash flow through the regular downturns, the avoidance of heavy long-term commitments to labour, and the avoidance of being locked into a particular production technology by heavy capital investment. The chief executive is likely to have accumulated a deep understanding of all aspects of an industry segment, and to have sources of information about that segment which are not easily accessible to others. Because of the OEM nature of most demand, a great deal of decision making in design and marketing is removed from the firm, leaving it to concentrate on production efficiency via the pursuit of cost cutting and cost avoidance. The structures of firms reflect their commonly small size and their concern with the control of production efficiency and they display relatively low levels of formalisation, specialisation and standardisation except in the management of core processes.[19] They are inevitably highly centralised, nepotistic and paternalistic in culture. Rivalry is intense and stems mainly from the large number of choices of supplier available to the buyers and buying agencies managing the OEM interface. The process is intensified further by the availability of detailed and sophisticated information on sources via government agencies such as the Trade Development Council and the Department of Industry, via private sources such as the stable of specialised buying guides published by Trade Media Ltd, or by buying agencies which also act as information hubs. The most obvious first point in considering the relevance of Porter's analysis in the light of the structure of Hong Kong's successful industries is that the firm as the prime unit of analysis begins to evaporate and be replaced by a loose network of allied firms. To whom then does strategic advice apply? This point will be returned to.

Factor Conditions

For fashion garment manufacture and niche market electronics to emerge as industries competitive in world terms, the key factor inputs are:

(i) design which relates to demand in target markets;
(ii) labour skills;
(iii) production technology able to service fast-moving changes of demand at low cost.

Design related to market demand has not been a Hong Kong strength for two reasons. Firstly, geographical distance from main markets in Europe and North America is capped by a cultural distance of factories making goods their workers would never use, such as an executive toy, or a silk blouse designed for Madison Avenue or the Champ Elysées. Secondly, the smallness of the firms and their low capitalisation mean that local R&D is avoided. The resulting importation of design and market sensitivity is arguably *not* a component of the Hong Kong environment unless it be argued that the means of facilitating their entry are local and the eventual source of it is irrelevant. This nevertheless introduces another blurring of conceptual boundaries, this time over the environmental boundary. Design sensitivity is not locally available but is made available. To what extent then is it part of the Hong Kong environment? Skilled or skillable, labour is unquestionably available in Hong Kong, and this may be attributed to three local conditions. The influx of refugees and their children from China in the 1940s and 1950s created a large pool of labour seeking industrial work, in the absence of alternatives in agriculture or until recently in the service sector. The characteristics of diligence, intelligence and perseverance needed for the successful acquisition of new skills are commonly attributed to people brought up within the Confucian ethic, stressing as it does the value of learning, social order, and obligation to family as a means of earning income via hard work, the resulting income being pooled.[20]

The third local condition affecting skilled labour has been government policy on education. This has stressed universal high-quality primary education, leaving secondary and tertiary education to be supported privately as well as publicly.[21] Public expenditure on tertiary education has stressed the acquisition of vocational skills, especially in fields related to production. The founding of two polytechnics, plus a University of Science and Technology, has added to the vocational bias of the two existing universities to produce a highly pragmatic looking tertiary sector. The last of the main necessary factor inputs, that of flexible, low-cost production technology, is a reflection partly of local skills emanating from the tertiary sector just described and partly from the openness of Hong Kong to information about externally available production machinery. The industry knowledge of chief executives includes where best to obtain production technology, but sources of supply will be outside Hong Kong in most cases. Again, it is arguable whether this can be classified as a local factor condition or not.

Related and Supporting Industries

It has been argued earlier that the prime unit of coordination in these highly successful industries is the network of connected firms, not the single firm itself. We find ourselves with an *explanans* serving as an *explanandum*. The passion for categorisation which serves Porter so well causes some artificiality in the argument when an enforced separation results from the assumption that the firm, somehow disembodied from its context, is capable of separate analysis. In Hong Kong, it is the industrial structure itself which causes the competitiveness at least as much as the firm itself. Given that caveat, it is a fact that related and supporting industries have played a crucial part in the success of fashion garments and niche market electronics. Local supplies of components in electronics and of fabrics, dyestuffs, accessories and labels in fashion have all made possible fast response and flexibility. Enhanced by low transaction costs due to culturally derived traditions of trust-bonding, and tight geographical concentration, the power of supporting industries to assist with eventual competitiveness must be rated highly.

Demand Conditions

Porter's main argument in terms of demand conditions is based on the assumption of home demand pressurising local firms to innovate faster and achieve more sophisticated competitive advantages. The mechanism is for home demand to give 'local firms a clearer or earlier picture of buyer needs than foreign rivals can have'.[22] He cites as an example the highly sophisticated Japanese consumption of electronic goods as an influence on Japanese abilities to wrest the television making industry away from US producers. In the fashion garment industry, where Hong Kong's main rival is Italy, it could be argued that Italian consumer sophistication is a major stimulus to local industrial competitiveness. And yet to all intents and purposes there is no home demand to speak of in Hong Kong for the products of its two major industries. Rejects and production over-runs in the fashion industry admittedly keep large numbers of tourists and locals happy, but the main production is all for long-distance export. The influence of demand comes via professional bulk buyers, not consumers. Trends and customer perceptions are not perceived directly but are filtered and interpolated. Perhaps this is a more efficient form of influence, but it is not what Porter meant. One must conclude, then, that either Hong Kong is handicapped by the lack of this supporting corner of the diamond, or that it is not a universally relevant contributor to the case for such strategic supports in the environment. Given the world success of these Hong Kong industries, it is hard to accept that the 'demand conditions' corner of the diamond is as important as Porter contends if they can succeed so dramatically without its benefits.

Chance

Porter sensibly includes a role for chance in his model and given Hong Kong's nature as something of a historical accident – a borrowed place on borrowed time – it is appropriate to consider the role of chance in stimulating its competitive success in the two principal industries under consideration here. Arguably, the following key elements are the result of fortune:

1. A combination of British legal infrastructure and government administration with an especially entreprenurial refugee population seeking an orderly society in which to accumulate family wealth.
2. The influx of managerial and technical skills acquired under Japanese influence[23] by Shanghainese industrialists, who brought them to Hong Kong in the 1950s and established the textile industries which in turn support the garment industry.

3. The change of government policy in China post-1979, which has fostered the opening up of a huge new labour market and maintained investment in Hong Kong as an industrial centre and a headquarters city.
4. The outward-looking orientation of most Hong Kong people caused by fears associated with 1997, which has led to very large numbers of Hong Kong students being educated in the West at university level, often in subjects related to the applied sciences such as engineering and electronics. Two subsidiary factors here are the urge to return as entrepreneurs, and the apparent natural aptitude for such subjects.
5. The Hong Kong government's policy for economic development is one of 'positive non-intervention', which means it provides good infrastructure but stays well away from business decisions. *Laissez-faire* rules. This may not be entirely a 'chance' factor, but it was established against the trend, long before it was internationally fashionable. It contrasts strongly with the interventionist alternative of Singapore's industrial policy, now argued to be taking Singapore incautiously and inefficiently beyond its level of industrial maturity.[24]

For a model to include the element of chance means risking the validity of the model itself if the chance elements build up to a powerful set of determinants. There would appear to be an argument here for Hong Kong being a special case to which the model applies but not completely, the chance factors being so powerful.

EXPLANATIONS OUTSIDE THE PORTER MODEL

The Role of China

A more serious dilemma in using Porter's model is posed by assumptions about the nation-state as the envelope within which certain consistencies are predictable. Conceptual problems stem from this in the Hong Kong case. Hong Kong has increasingly behaved as though the border with China was not relevant, and the wholesale movement of production facilities in Guangdong, Shenzhen and, to a lesser extent, Shanghai and Fujian has made it impossible to study an industry segment inside one national envelope. Both electronics and garments live in two environments and appear to do so successfully, albeit with different balances of how much is located in each. Nation states and their policies may be seen here as overlapping sets of influences and not as single sets. The model is necessarily much more complex than Porter would suggest. A dilemma arises if one says that China and Hong Kong are becoming one state anyway so this conflation is only temporary. But, in practice, they are following a policy of one country, two systems, and are so different in nature that it will still be necessary after 1997 to see their environments as separate. Currently they are two but in business practice treated as one; whereas, in future, they will be one but only properly analysable as two.

Different Strategies in Electronics and Fashion

In order to explain why fashion garment manufacturing has tended to stay in Hong Kong whereas electronics has tended more to move inland into China, it is interesting to bring to the account the play of forces in Porter's diamond. Perhaps the most critical factor condition is labour, closely followed by land. In the case of electronics there is more of a need for low-cost labour, because the standardisation of production technology means that competition can come from almost anywhere, and certainly in the region from Malaysia, Indonesia, Philippines, Thailand as well as other provinces of China. It follows that the transfer into China to avoid Hong Kong's high labour costs is inevitable. Space for factory production lines is also needed and in chronically short supply in Hong Kong. In fashion garments, labour is an important factor, but so too is design craftmanship, a feature which is much harder to release outside the Hong Kong context. Nor are space needs so critical, as long production line systems are used less in this industry, and small facilities are common. Most critical is the maintenance of the small enterprise network as the base on which to offer customers the high speed of response for which this industry segment in Hong Kong is renowned. This brings into account both firm structure and demand conditions. Electronics have tended to move out of Hong Kong and fashion garments have tended to stay. Changing factor conditions have led to a rational relocation of industry. In the case of electronics, the match of input factors with needs is better, whereas it is demand conditions that have exerted pressure on garments to stay in Hong Kong. Traditional firm structures and interaction with related industries have played a part in conditioning the responses. Porter's model is usable in explaining the discrepant behaviour of the two industries, and it fosters an understanding of how competitiveness is eventually sought differently in each case. For electronics, the primary weapon is price, and, in fashion garments, it is responsiveness, and this difference of emphasis is enough to lead to variance in location strategy. In neither case, however, does Porter's main argument about demand conditions apply: namely that the home market sophistication leads to industry progress.

Alternative Explanations

The World Bank's recent study of economic growth and public policy in the miracle economies of East Asia[25] proposes another diamond. In this, the four key elements are given as:

1. Macro-economic stability;
2. Human capital formation;
3. Openness to international trade; and
4. An environment encouraging private investment and competition.

The same report identifies the success of Hong Kong's economy as a whole with its ability to stick to certain 'fundamentals' and these are more specific, operational versions of the above factors. What they amount to is:

(i) a stable macroeconomy;
(ii) high human capital;
(iii) effective and secure financial systems;
(iv) the limiting of price distortions;
(v) openness to foreign technology; and
(vi) agricultural development policies.

It must be acknowledged immediately that the kind of normative theory developed within the World Bank is designed to apply at the level of national political economy and not at the level of industry segment. A direct comparison with Porter is therefore inappropriate. At the same time some useful critical insight may be gained by looking at the contrast between the kind of efficiency determinants of concern in the context of economic *development*, and the assumptions which lie behind Porter's diamond which perhaps unconsciously reflect the context of large advanced economies with well-developed industries.

Porter appears to assume the stability of fairly advanced economies and gives few examples of small countries subject to the extreme dependence and extreme volatility evident in the case of Hong Kong. His main book[26] considers Italy, Sweden, Japan, Switzerland, Germany, Britain and the US, with only Korea representing the developing context. In the field of human capital, there is clearly much in common between Porter and the World Bank report. The role of effective and secure financial systems is discussed by Porter almost exclusively in terms of capital markets and the instruments used within them. This approach ignores alternative means of capital formation and acquisition common in Pacific Asia, namely the private market for investment in the small and medium sector and network funding within large business groups. This ethnocentric bias in Porter does not necesarily invalidate his larger point about the finance factor's place in the model, but it ignores the process inherent in alternative business systems and the indigenous mechanisms underlying competitiveness.

With regard to the limiting of price distortions and openness to foreign technology, we see forces at work which produce a level playing field. Both the World Bank's account and Porter's model advocating firm rivalry point to the central importance of this feature for stimulating competitive improvement and innovation. But an interesting qualification may be worth examining and it is that the perfect market may, in Hong Kong, only apply in certain domains. This is despite the widespread assumption that Hong Kong is the ultimate case of *laissez-faire* capitalism. Govenment licensing limits competition in the supply of telecommunications and power, and price fixing is implemented in public transport. Food has for decades been a matter of hidden subsidy from China. Land and property are made available from a government monopoly, and a committee of bankers establishes interest rates. It is perhaps only in the domain of technology imports, labour skills and the production process itself that competition is actually pure, thus raising the question of limits to the areas of an economy where competitive rivalry should be intense.

HONG KONG AND THE PORTER MODEL

Eight issues emerge from an analysis of Hong Kong. None of them challenges Porter's model in any fundamental sense because the model's elasticity makes that impossible. Yet they do raise warnings about sensitivity in its use outside the context of large developed economies. The crucial points are:

1. The firm as the ultimate unit of analysis is hard to reconcile with the networked economic structures of much Asian business. Related to that, can the structure of supporting industry, a critical corner of Porter's diamond, be used as a major determinant when understanding of the firm requires seeing it as a network hub? Cause and effect become inseparable.
2. When a factor like design technology or machinery is easily imported, can it be considered a local factor?
3. How significant is the 'demand conditions' corner of the diamond if it has no relevance to Hong Kong's most competitive industries? Should it be redefined to mean more than sophisticated home market demand.
4. The role of chance seems to loom very large in the Hong Kong case and to qualify the model's value.
5. Assumptions about the salience of the nation-state as a valid envelope are very hard to reconcile with Hong Kong's position vis-a-vis China, and with its extreme openness to flows of capital, technology, labour and material.
6. The normative assumptions about a stable macro-economy do not accord with the Hong Kong experience.
7. The normative assumptions about perfect competition do not accord with the Hong Kong experience, despite much stereotypical thinking to the contrary.

8. Systems of capital formation vary substantially across the world's business systems, and do not always follow Western norms, procedures, or visibility. In particular, Asian versions may inhibit true competition, as the 'irrational' workings of many stock markets in the region suggest.

While there can be no doubt that Porter's attempt to deal with the longitudinal problem of fostering the emergence of competitive industry segments is the most fully worked out to date, it is perhaps natural that the large generalisations entailed will separate it from much detailed reality. It was clearly researched in advanced economies with large home markets and a bias to manufacturing for export. It was not researched in small economies, in resource-based economies, or in non-traded sectors. It is inevitably partial. The case of Hong Kong displays the role of chance as a major factor, and shows that world competitiveness can be achieved without every element of Porter's diamond and with a two-part model, predicated on the importance of firm strategy, structure and rivalry, and of factor conditions. The example of Hong Kong suggests that Porter's theory should take account of a greater variety of contexts in order to amend and improve claims of generality.

NOTES

1. S.G. Redding, 'Comparative Management Theory: Jungle, Zoo or Fossil Bed', in *Organisation Studies* (in press).
2. M.E. Porter, *The Competitive Advantage of Nations* (London, 1990).
3. R.D. Whitley, *Business Systems in East Asia: Firms, Markets and Societies* (London, 1992).
4. P. Yetton, *et al.*, 'Are Diamonds a Country's Best Friend? A Critique of Porter's Theory of National Competition as Applied to Canada, New Zealand and Australia', *Australian Journal of Management* Vol.17, No.1 (1992), pp.89–119.
5. Yetton, 'Are Diamonds . . .', p.118.
6. S.G. Redding, *The Spirit of Chinese Capitalism* (New York, 1990); S. Tam and S.G. Redding, 'The Impact of Colonialism on the Formation of an Entrepreneurial Society in Hong Kong' in S. Birley and I.C. Macmillan (eds.), *Entrepreneurship Research: Global Perspectives* (Amsterdam, 1993).
7. Business and Professionals Federation of Hong Kong, *Hong Kong 21: A Ten Year Vision and Agenda for Hong Kong's Economy* (Hong Kong, 1993).
8. BPFHK, *Hong Kong 21*, p.21.
9. S. Chiu and T.L. Lui, 'Industrial Restructuring in Hong Kong: Implications for Production and Employment Strategies', Conference Paper, 11 Oct. 1993, Centre of Asian Studies, University of Hong Kong.
10. Chiu and Lui, 'Industrial Restructuring . . .', p.24.
11. Ibid. p.13.
12. M.E. Porter, *Competitive Advantage: Creating and Sustaining Superior Performance* (London, 1985).
13. Porter, *Competitive Advantage of Nations*.
14. M.E. Porter, 'Towards a Dynamic Theory of Strategy', *Strategic Management Journal* Vol.12 (1991), p.95.
15. Porter, 'Towards . . .', p.109.
16. T.C. Chou, 'The Experience of SME's Development in Taiwan: High Export

Contribution and Export-Intensity', *Rivista Internazionale de Scienze Economische e Commerciali*, Vol.39, No.12 (1992), pp.1067–84.
17. Redding, *The Spirit*.
18. S.G. Redding, 'Weak Organisations and Strong Linkages: Managerial Ideology and Chinese Family Business Networks', in G.G. Hamilton, (ed.), *Business Networks and Economic Development in East and South East Asia* (Hong Kong 1991), pp.30–47; and 'Societal Transformation and the Contribution of Authority Relations and Cooperation Norms in Overseas Chinese Business', in W.M. Tu (ed.), *Confucian Traditions in East Asian Modernity* (in press).
19. Redding, *The Spirit*.
20. J. Salaff, *Working Daughters of Hong Kong* (Cambridge, 1981).
21. World Bank, *The East Asian Miracle* (New York, 1993).
22. Porter, *Competitive Advantage of Nations*, p.86.
23. J.M. Nishida, 'The Japanese Influence on the Shanghainese Textile Industry and Implications for Hong Kong', (M.Phil., Hong Kong, 1990).
24. Hong Kong Centre for Economic Research, *HKCER Letters*, No.15 (1992).
25. World Bank, *East Asian*.
26. Porter, *Competitive Advantage of Nations*.

The Competitive Advantage of Taiwan

LAWRENCE J. LAU

1. INTRODUCTION

In his monumental study, *The Competitive Advantage of Nations*, Michael Porter distinguishes between the concepts of what he calls 'competitive advantage' and the more traditional 'comparative advantage' of David Ricardo. Competitive advantage, according to Porter, is defined at the level of the industry, or industry segment, and is identifiable through a dominant or significant share of the world export market of that particular industry or industry segment. More specifically, Porter uses the following empirical measurements as working indicators of competitiveness: 'International competitive advantage is measured as either (1) the presence of substantial and sustained exports to a wide array of other nations and/or (2) significant outbound foreign investment based on skills and assets created in the home country.'[1] In Porter's framework, competitive advantage applies typically to a cluster of related industries. The clustering of a group of industries is important from the point of view of competitive advantage because of the existence of externalities and economies of scale. These economies arise because of user–supplier relationships and because of knowledge and skill complementarities across industries. For example, there are considerable knowledge, skill and technological complementarities among the manufacturing of photocopiers, fax machines, printers, and scanners. In practice, competitive advantage in a particular industry in a particular country in Porter's study is largely indicated through that country's market share in total world exports of the industry. Other measures of competitive advantage are, of course, possible – for example, the number of new products introduced, the number of patents,[2] the quantity of new investment or new capacity, and increase in productivity. Expansion, or maintenance, of the export share in the world market in a given industry, or industry segment, is an important indicator of on-going innovative activity. Expansion or maintenance of the export share is only possible if new production is being created and new markets are being developed. The product *per se* may not be necessarily innovative from the point of view of the world; however, the industry segment must be regarded as innovative relative to the home country in the sense that it is new or expanding. Porter associates competitive advantage with increases in productivity. However, since labour productivity – the average output per unit of labour – can be made

---

Lawrence J. Lau, Stanford University, California

arbitrarily high by increasing capital per unit labour, the appropriate measure of productivity to focus on is not so much labour productivity as the productivity of capital, or alternatively, total factor productivity – the increase in output while holding inputs constant. The use of capital productivity appears especially appropriate because of the mobility of capital across countries. Capital is deployed and moved, not by nations or governments, or even by industries, but by firms, to wherever it is the most productive – that is, has the highest rate of return. Thus, the inflow of foreign direct investment in a particular industry or industry segment can be regarded as another indicator of competitiveness. Measured in this way, the Unites States is actually quite competitive in many high-technology sectors because of the foreign direct investment in both manufacturing and R&D activities that it has been able to attract to these industries.

Porter also addresses the issue of whether it makes sense to speak of the 'competitive advantage' of a nation. It appears that one can extend Porter's criterion of 'the presence of substantial and sustained exports to a wide array of other nations' to apply to a nation in the aggregate, even though he himself does not do so. If a country's share in total world exports is significant, and has been increasing, or at least held constant, over time, that country may be regarded as possessing competitive advantage in the aggregate. This is because the aggregate export share can be substantial and increasing only if the export shares in some industries are substantial and increasing. A sustained substantial export share in the aggregate is therefore indicative of the presence of competitive advantage in the aggregate.[3] In a highly competitive environment, with ever shifting competitive advantages, even keeping the aggregate export share constant requires continuous deployment of resources from old declining industries to new expanding industries. It should be noted that the meaning of 'competitiveness' in Porter's definition connotes the opposite of what economists, at least neo-classical economists, traditionally mean by competitiveness. For example, a firm producing a product with a strong brand name recognition and hence consumer loyalty, such as Coca-Cola, or MacDonald's, obviously has a competitive advantage according to Porter's definition. But strong brand names may actually be anti-competitive in the classical sense – they give the firms too much market power and reduce consumer welfare. This is also related to the question of the proportion of profit that is due to 'rent' rather than creation of value.

In Porter's study, two newly industrialised countries, Singapore and South Korea, were originally included. Taiwan was not. However, in the book, Singapore is mentioned only in passing, even though it was part of the original study. One is left wondering why. South Korea is very different from Singapore, and even though it is at a comparable stage of development as Taiwan, it has a significantly different industrial structure with a much higher concentration. Korean industrial enterprises tend to be much larger, and more capital intensive, than those in Taiwan. The objective of this paper is to explore the applicability of Porter's framework of analysis to Taiwan's historical experience.

In addition to export shares in the world market, are there other useful indicators of (rising) competitive advantage in selected industries in a newly industrialised country such as Taiwan? We can identify a few.

First, when firms begin to promote and market under their own brand names and attempt to shift from being simply a subcontractor or an OEM supplier, it is a sign that they are ready to compete aggressively in the world market. Not many firms in Taiwan have been able to make this transition. The examples include Acer (microcomputers), Giant (bicycles) and Kennex (tennis rackets).[4] Attempting to establish one's own brand name is an enormous undertaking because it reflects a relatively long-term commitment to develop in-house design and R&D capabilities, which also implies that firms begin to have a vested interest in having intellectual property rights safeguarded and enforced. In the 1950s, Japanese manufactured goods, including automobiles, were generally considered poor quality. At that time, 'Made in Japan' connoted something inexpensive but flimsy. In fact, a small town in Japan actually renamed itself 'usa' so that it can label its products 'made in usa', in the hope that the potential purchasers will mistake them as having been made in the USA. It is only relatively recently, since the 1970s, that Japanese-made products have acquired a reputation of being 'innovative' and 'high-quality' and competitive advantage can be gained or lost over a relatively short span of time.

Second, firms will begin to have an increasingly higher ratio of value-added to gross value in their exports. One of the problems of using the export share as an empirical indicator is that it fails to distinguish the value-added in the exports by the exporting country from the gross value of exports. For the same gross value of exports, and hence the same export share, there can be an enormous range of value-added. A country that adds little value acts very much like a subcontractor and does not have much competitive advantage despite large nominal quantities of exports. For example, Malaysia is the world's largest exporter of semi-conductors (as well as the largest importer of semiconductors), but few would argue that it has a competitive advantage, in the Porter sense, in the manufacture of semiconductors. A rising ratio of value-added to gross value in exports is indicative of increasing capabilities and hence also of rising competitive advantage.

In section 2, we review briefly the economic success story of Taiwan. That Taiwan has been successful few would argue, although one may differ with regard to the future prospects. In section 3, we explore whether Taiwan did have a competitive advantage, in the sense of Porter. In section 4, we examine the factors for Taiwan's success and its competitiveness. Some concluding remarks are made in section 5.

2. THE ECONOMIC RECORD

Taiwan is one of the few countries that has managed to transform its economy from a backward agricultural one to a newly industrialised one in the post-war period. Its success is often referred to as a 'miracle'.[5] Gross national product (GNP) per capita in Taiwan rose more than 60-fold from US$145 in 1951 to US$8,813 in 1991.[6] In real terms, GNP and GNP per capita in Taiwan grew at average annual rates of approximately 9.2 and 7.1 per cent respectively in the three decades from 1962 to 1991 (see Table

TABLE 1
REAL GNP AND REAL GNP PER CAPITA OF TAIWAN

Year	Real GNP(billion 1990 US$)		Real GNP per Capita(1990 US$)	
	GNP	Growth Rate	GNP/Capita	Growth Rate
1951	5.88		713	
1952	6.64	12.93%	778	9.15%
1953	7.27	9.52%	824	5.84%
1954	7.92	8.86%	868	5.33%
1955	8.57	8.24%	905	4.29%
1956	8.97	4.73%	914	1.07%
1957	9.63	7.27%	951	3.99%
1958	10.29	6.91%	985	3.57%
1959	11.04	7.27%	1023	3.83%
1960	11.72	6.16%	1052	2.83%
1961	12.49	6.59%	1086	3.30%
1962	13.59	8.81%	1148	5.62%
1963	15.08	10.95%	1236	7.74%
1964	17.08	13.27%	1360	10.03%
1965	18.47	8.14%	1430	5.15%
1966	20.17	9.17%	1520	6.26%
1967	22.38	10.98%	1645	8.26%
1968	24.50	9.48%	1759	6.90%
1969	26.99	10.15%	1894	7.68%
1970	30.10	11.51%	2068	9.21%
1971	33.93	12.75%	2285	10.47%
1972	38.53	13.55%	2547	11.47%
1973	43.01	11.62%	2791	9.55%
1974	42.35	-1.53%	2698	-3.30%
1975	44.21	4.40%	2766	2.50%
1976	51.05	15.46%	3129	13.14%
1977	56.14	9.98%	3373	7.79%
1978	62.96	12.14%	3713	10.08%
1979	68.01	8.02%	3933	5.93%
1980	71.08	4.52%	4033	2.54%
1981	74.94	5.43%	4175	3.51%
1982	78.90	5.27%	4316	3.39%
1983	86.26	9.33%	4643	7.58%
1984	96.54	11.92%	5120	10.27%
1985	102.46	6.14%	5360	4.68%
1986	118.84	15.98%	6145	14.65%
1987	134.31	13.02%	6872	11.83%
1988	143.92	7.15%	7280	5.94%
1989	154.38	7.26%	7724	6.10%
1990	161.55	4.65%	7994	3.49%
1991	173.75	7.55%	8507	6.43%

1).[7] To put this performance in perspective, we may note that during the two decades of the most rapid economic growth in the history of the United States (approximately 1870–90), real GNP grew at a rate of approximately five per cent per annum.[8] Of all other countries, only Japan (1955–76) and South Korea (1965–the present) ever experienced a comparable rate of real economic growth over as long a period.[9] The growth in the real output of Taiwan during this period was accompanied by a steady growth of factor inputs. Between 1953 and 1990, the gross fixed capital stock, employment, labour hours and human capital[10] grew at average annual rates of 12.1, 2.8, 2.5 and 2.8 per cent per annum respectively.[11] Of these inputs, physical capital has been found to be overwhelmingly the most important sources of economic growth in Taiwan during this period, accounting for three-quarters of the increase in real output.[12] The paramount importance of tangible capital accumulation has also been observed by Moses Abramovitz for US economic growth during the late 19th and early 20th centuries. Growth in real private consumption per capita has not kept pace with the growth in real GNP per capita. Between 1965 and 1990, while real GNP per capita of Taiwan increased fivefold, private real consumption per capita increased not quite fourfold, implying a significant increase in the proportion of national output saved. In Figure 1, the savings ratio (gross national savings divided by GNP) is plotted against real GNP per capita. It is clear that there is a positive, linear relationship between the savings ratio and real GNP per capita at low levels of real GNP per capita (below US$3,000 in 1990 prices). As real GNP per capita increased beyond the threshold level, the savings ratio stabilises at an average of approximately 35 per cent, a remarkably high rate by the standards of the world. As the national savings ratio rose, domestic investment grew by leaps and bounds. Since the mid-1960s, domestic investment in Taiwan was almost entirely financed by national savings. There was no foreign aid and relatively little foreign investment or loan. With the high investment rate, the capital stock of Taiwan grew at approximately 12 per cent per annum. By comparison, the capital stocks of the advanced industrial economies, except Japan, grew at average annual rates of less than five per cent during the same period. It is the ready availability of investment capital that enables the firms in Taiwan to enhance their competitive advantage.

As a result of export promotion policy, which consisted of preferential tax treatment and credit subsidies, rebates of customs duties for re-exported intermediate goods and raw materials, and maintenance of an appropriate exchange rate, the growth of exports in both nominal and real terms were nothing short of being phenomenal. Between 1962 and 1991, the value of exports in US dollars increased by 22 per cent per annum and real exports increased by 16 per cent per annum. The export sector has grown from approximately ten per cent of GNP in 1960 to more than 60 per cent in 1991, and the strong effect which export growth has had on the growth of the real GNP of the Taiwan economy is evident.

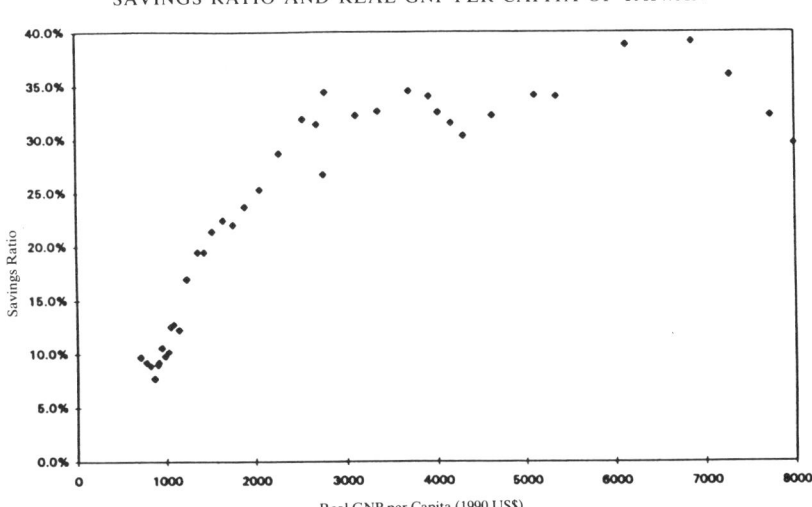

FIGURE 1

SAVINGS RATIO AND REAL GNP PER CAPITA OF TAIWAN

In the 1960s, Taiwan adopted a system of floating exchange rates which turned out to be *de facto* a system of managed rates. The exchange rate was maintained within a ten per cent band for more than two decades. However, since September 1985, when the exchange rate stood at NT$40.40 per US$, it appreciated continuously, to almost 25.00. Recently, it stood at 26.50. Overall, the exchange rate has risen almost 40 per cent with respect to the US dollar. Despite the appreciation, the export share, at least in the aggregate, has continued to hold.

The growth in output in Taiwan was achieved through a very rapid and substantial growth in labour productivity, through improvements in the average productivity of labour (in terms of real GDP – or, equivalently, value added – per labour hour), the capital intensity (in terms of physical capital per labour hour) and human capital intensity (in terms of years of schooling per person in the working age population of 15 to 64 years inclusive). Over the period 1953–90, it is apparent that output per labour hour increased more than seven times, spurred by the increase in capital intensity, which increased approximately 60 times, and in human capital intensity, which approximately doubled. It is the increase in the physical capital per unit labour, sometimes referred to as 'capital deepening', that has allowed the firms and industries in Taiwan to upgrade continually and to introduce new processes and new products in order to maintain their competitive advantage. The increase in human capital intensity is no less important, as physical capital and human capital are in fact complementary.[13] It does not do any good to have sophisticated equipment if educated and skilled labour cannot be found to operate the equipment effectively.

In Figure 2, output per labour hour is plotted against physical capital per labour hour. It is clear that there is a positive relationship between the two: higher capital intensity leads to higher labour productivity. One may also note that the relationship tends to flatten at higher and higher capital intensities – in other words, it takes more and more additional capital per unit labour to achieve a given increase in output per unit labour. This is the 'law of diminishing returns' at work. The strategy of 'capital deepening' has almost run its course; or, in Porter's terminology, the 'investment-driven' phase is almost over. Future increases in labour productivity will have to come increasingly from what economists call 'technical progress' or 'total factor productivity', or 'innovation' in Porter's terminology, which depends on such intangible 'capital' as 'R&D capital' and institutional and organisational capabilities. Finally, in Figure 3, we compare the average productivity of physical capital (output per unit of the capital stock) across four newly industrialised countries: Hong Kong, Singapore, South Korea and Taiwan. We see that capital productivity in Korea and Taiwan has remained higher, although it fell quite rapidly in both cases in the decades before 1980. This provides further evidence that Taiwan must begin to rely on 'innovation' as a major source of further growth.

FIGURE 2

THE RELATIONSHIP BETWEEN THE AVERAGE PRODUCTIVITY IN LABOUR AND CAPITAL INTENSITY

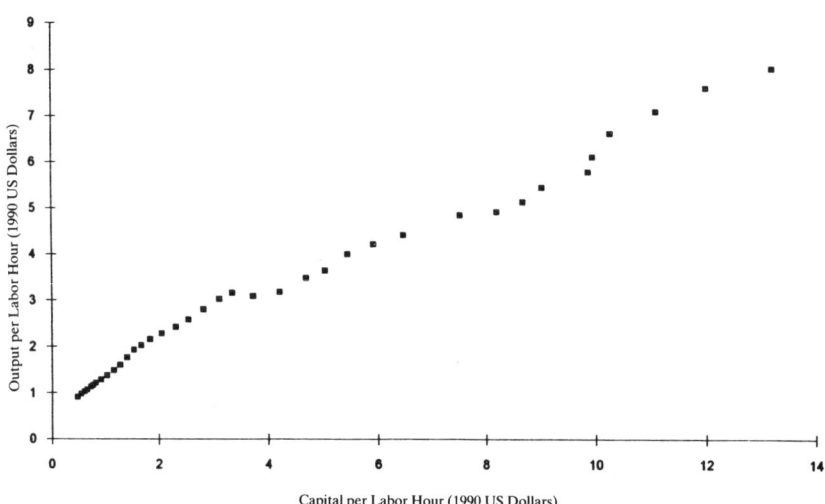

FIGURE 3
THE PRODUCTIVITY OF CAPITAL (OUTPUT PER UNIT OF CAPITAL)

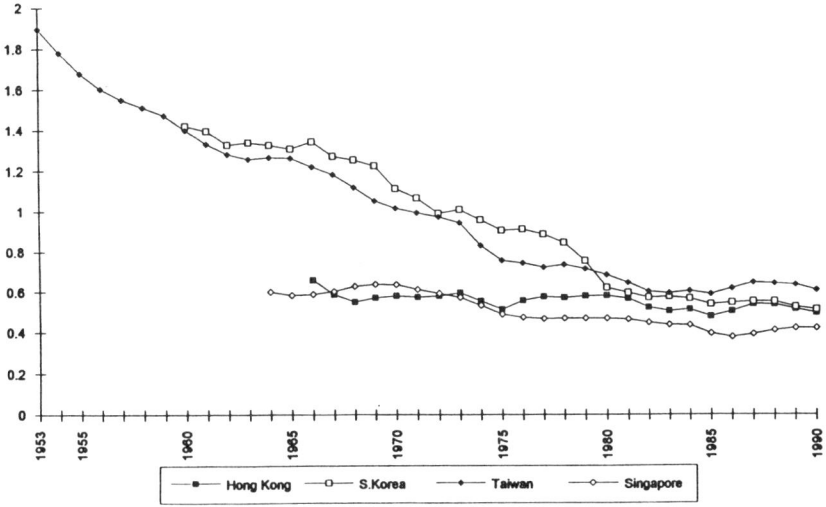

3. DID TAIWAN HAVE A COMPETITIVE ADVANTAGE?

While exports have led Taiwan's economic growth, the exports, as well as the export industries, have undergone significant transformations. The initial exports were mostly agriculturally based, such as bananas and sugar. Subsequently, the dominant exports became processed agricultural products, such as canned asparagus and mushrooms. Then it was dominated heavily by textiles, including garments, and then by shoes and handbags. When the new Taiwan dollar began to appreciate in 1986, many of the traditional export industries in Taiwan, such as textiles and shoes, were no longer competitive in the world market and were forced to either close down, contract drastically, or move offshore to countries with lower labour costs. The necessity of industrial upgrading became obvious. New product lines were developed, sometimes with government assistance. For example, bicycles, personal computers, and notebook computers have come to replace the traditional exports. Taiwan was at one time or another the largest exporter of canned mushrooms and shoes to the world; it is currently the largest exporter of bicycles and the second largest exporter of notebook computers. If indeed Taiwan has any competitive advantage, it has been changing continuously and rapidly. Michael Porter emphasises, quite rightly, that the concept of competitive advantage applies to firms, and perhaps to industries, but not to nations *per se*. However, finely disaggregated international trade data for Taiwan are not readily available, either in Taiwan or in standard international sources. The available disaggregated international trade data are unfortunately not classified in the same way as the standard international trade classification. Consequently, it has not been possible to replicate Porter's general method in the case of Taiwan. Instead, we look at three different types of data, including those pertaining to the aggregate economy as a whole.

We first look at the aggregate exports of Taiwan as a share of total world exports and use it as a gauge for competitiveness in the aggregate. If Taiwan is losing competitive advantage as a whole, then one would expect its share of the world market to decline. This aggregate trade share also reflects the ingenuity and flexibility of Taiwanese firms in adjusting to changes in business conditions and opening and developing new commodities and new markets for export. The share of Taiwan's exports in total world exports was – at less than 0.25 per cent – quite low and stable between 1952 and 1962. It then climbed steadily from about 1962, and except for a temporary decline due to the first oil crisis, the rise in Taiwan's export share continued unabated until 1987, when the new Taiwan dollar was revalued upwards by almost 40 per cent relative to the US dollar. Since then, however, Taiwan's share of the world's exports has remained steady at slightly less than 2.5 per cent. By this measure, the overall competitive advantage of Taiwan appears to have held steady in the past several years as its export industries have managed to hold on to their market shares. Of course the aggregate picture may mask many significant developments – in particular, individual industries may gain or lose even as the aggregate export share remains constant. We therefore examine next the changes in 'competitiveness' in the computer and computer peripheral equipment industry. In Table 2, we present the five most important products of the computer and computer peripheral industry in Taiwan for every other year in the decade since 1984. Table 2 shows that, over time, printers, disk drives, and terminals have gradually been supplanted by microcomputers, monitors, motherboards and power supplies – indicating rising technological sophistication and progress from lower value-added products to higher value-added products. In Table 3, we present Taiwan's share of the world market in selected products in this industry. It shows a pattern of extremely rapid growth from a totally insignificant to a dominant market position in a matter of years. For example, Taiwan now has more than half of the world market in scanners and more than 80 per cent of the world market in mice. If the overseas production of Taiwan firms are included, the share of the world market in monitors and keyboards both increase to 47 per cent. This conforms to the pattern, identified by Porter, of 'significant outbound foreign investment based on skills and assets created in the home country', and is thus also indicative of competitive advantage. Tables 2 and 3 also provide empirical confirmation of the 'clustering' hypothesis advanced by Porter.

TABLE 2

THE FIVE MOST IMPORTANT INFORMATION INDUSTRY PRODUCTS IN TAIWAN BY GROSS VALUE OF ANNUAL PRODUCTION

Rank	1984	1986	1988	1990	1992
1	Terminal	Monitor	Microcomputer	Monitor	Monitor
2	Microcomputer	Microcomputer	Monitor	Microcomputer	Microcomputer
3	Monitor	Terminal	Motherboard	Motherboard	Motherboard
4	Disk Drive	Disk Drive	Terminal	Power Supply	Terminal
5	Printer	Printer	Power Supply	Terminal	Power Supply

Source: Information Industry Institute, Taipei, Taiwan, Republic of China, reported in *Tien-Hsia*, 1 Dec. 1993, p.110, Table, 2.

TABLE 3

TAIWAN'S SHARE OF THE WORLD MARKET IN SELECTED INFORMATION INDUSTRY PRODUCTS (PERCENTAGE)

Product	1984	1986	1988	1990	1992
Terminal	22	30	32	24	24
Monitor	28	34	31	32	42
Personal Computer	5	8	10	10	11
Keyboard	negl.	31	26	36	26
Mouse	negl.	negl.	35	72	80
Scanner	negl.	20	26	35.3	50.4

Note: negl. = negligible.
Source: Information Industry, Taipei, Taiwan, Republic of China, reported in *Tien-Hsia*, December 1, 1993, p.110, Table 3.

However, it is worthwhile to make the distinction between selling a product under one's own brand name and being an OEM supplier. The latter generally has low profit margins and little or no market power. In this regard, Taiwan's computer and computer peripheral equipment industry still consists predominantly of OEM-type suppliers and hence does not have a strong competitive advantage. The only well-known international brand name is that of Acer, which makes microcomputers. The personal computer industry in Taiwan also suffered, along with others in industrialised countries, from the world-wide recession and price-cutting in that industry. There are indications of declining market shares in certain, less technologically demanding product lines such as keyboards and terminals. Overall, the product life cycle in this industry is quite short and the competitive advantage of Taiwan is not too durable. It is a tribute to the ingenuity and flexibility of the firms in Taiwan that they have managed to keep ahead. In the mean time, the gross value of production of this industry has in ten years leaped from approximately US$400 million in 1983 to US$10.4 billion in 1993. (Considering that the unit prices of these products have been coming down steadily at approximately 14 per cent per year on average, the increase in value is all the more impressive.) It is now the leading export industry in Taiwan, having taken over from the more traditional industries of textiles, garments, shoes and umbrellas. In Table 4, Taiwan's shares of the three principal world markets – United States, Japan and the European Union – in ten selected products are reported for 1989–91. It is immediately apparent that these market shares shift markedly from year to year. For example, Taiwan's share in the light fixture and umbrellas and parasol markets of the United States declined by almost ten percentage points between 1989 and 1991. The decline in Taiwan's share of the umbrella and parasol markets in Japan and the European Community are even greater. For the older industries, such as artificial flowers and garments, Taiwan has low and declining world markets. In the more mature industries, such as toys, handbags, and shoes, Taiwan still holds significant market shares but they have continued to fall steadily. The zipper industry has just reached maturity and begun to decline. The bicycle industry, with 80 per cent of the US and Japanese markets and a rising share of the European market, is probably at or near the peak of its competitiveness, thanks to the successful development of composite material technology in Taiwan which has enabled manufacturers to move into the high end of the product line. At least one of the major manufacturers, Giant, has begun to promote its own brand of bicycles. The blinds industry, which has 90 per cent of of the US market, is showing signs of decline in the Japanese and European markets.

Thus for many of its industries, Taiwan clearly meets, or met at one time, the test of substantiality of exports in Porter's definition of competitiveness. However, it is less clear whether the exports in the individual industries are sustained enough to meet the requirement of Porter's definition, given the rapid turnovers of the product composition of its exports. Perhaps one has to reach the inevitable conclusion that in light manufacturing industries there is only transitory, but no permanent, competitive advantage. However, it is precisely this background of rapidly shifting competitive advantage which makes Taiwan's ability to increase or maintain its aggregate share of the total world export market all the more remarkable. Taiwan's competitive advantage lies in its ability to adjust rapidly to changing market, technological and competitive conditions.

4. ACCOUNTING FOR TAIWAN'S SUCCESS

What accounts for Taiwan's success? We shall structure our discussion in this section along the classification scheme employed by Porter in his study.

Factor Conditions

As we have seen in section 3, the growth in output in Taiwan in the postwar period is mostly due to the accumulation of tangible capital.

TABLE 4

TAIWAN'S SHARE OF THE PRINCIPAL WORLD MARKETS IN SELECTED PRODUCTS (PERCENTAGE)

Product	U.S.A.			Japan			European Union		
	1989	1990	1991	1989	1990	1991	1989	1990	1991
Blinds	93.4	83.9	92.1	87.9	65.0	57.6	19.2	20.8	16.1
Bicycle	76.5	79.2	78.1	80.7	86.1	87.9	24.4	29.4	32.7
Light fixture	49.5	38.8	40.7	35.0	23.8	28.0	4.9	4.0	5.0
Umbrella and parasol	44.5	25.0	35.8	74.1	47.7	32.7	25.0	13.2	13.5
Zipper and parts	32.6	28.0	31.9	87.8	70.0	69.5	11.5	9.6	9.5
Shoes	23.9	12.2	16.0	25.0	19.3	17.7	6.2	3.9	3.9
Travel products and handbags	21.8	15.8	18.3	7.4	5.6	5.7	12.9	8.9	8.0
Toy and indoor game equipment	13.5	11.4	10.5	20.8	17.4	16.1	7.0	5.2	4.9
Garment	11.7	10.3	9.7	9.4	5.3	4.2	1.3	1.0	1.2
Artificial flower, leaf and fruit	6.4	2.5	3.4	12.6	8.7	6.3	3.0	1.7	1.1

Source: Unpublished research of Professor P.C. Chen, Department of Economics, National Taiwan University, Taipei, Taiwan, Republic of China.

Approximately three-quarters of the growth of real output may be attributed to increases in physical capital input, 15 per cent to increases in the human capital input and the remaining ten per cent to increases in the labour input. In other words, the major part of Taiwan's economic success may be directly attributed to its high rates of savings and investment. In Table 5 we report the results of a growth accounting exercise carried out by Kim and Lau.[14] It shows that the most important source of economic growth for Taiwan, as well as for the other newly industrialised countries of Hong Kong, Singapore and South Korea, is physical capital accumulation, followed by human capital, but with technical progress (or equivalently, the increase of total factor productivity) playing no role. This is in contrast to the industrialised countries, in which technical progress is the most important, with the exception of Japan. This result is completely consistent with Porter's 'Four-Phase' sequence of economic development. The newly industrialised countries are still in the investment-driven phase, whereas the industrialised countries are in the 'innovation-driven' phase. The availablity of US aid was extremely critical to Taiwan in the 1950s. Subsequently, the high domestic savings ratio assured the ready availability of domestic capital. In addition, the supply of skilled manpower was relatively abundant, both because of the influx of people from mainland China in 1949 and because of the educational system put in place by the Japanese colonial government before 1945. The government in Taiwan continued to invest in education, and in particular extended first primary education, and then junior high education, universally. This provided a broad base of workers with skills appropriate for the level of economic development. The government also promoted technical vocational education. The result is a highly adaptable and trainable labour force. Total educational expenditure has been rising as a percentage of GNP over time, from approximately two per cent in 1961 to just under six in 1990. Human capital intensity has

TABLE 5
THE SOURCES OF ECONOMIC GROWTH OF SELECTED COUNTRIES
(PERCENTAGE)

	Capital	Labor	Human Capital	Technical Progress
Hong Kong	66	22	11	0
Singapore	63	25	13	0
S. Korean	67	19	14	0
Taiwan	75	14	11	0
France	33	-1	4	63
W. Germany	36	-7	5	66
Japan	48	6	3	43
U.K.	35	4	6	55
U.S.	23	30	4	43

increased: whereas in 1953 average years of attendance at education were three, in 1991 they were about nine. It is worth noting that only after the demand for basic education was satisfied did the government begin to increase significantly opportunities for tertiary education.[15] What should not be left unremarked is the large number of graduate students who went abroad, principally to the United States, to pursue advanced degrees from the 1950s. At its peak, the annual flow approached 20,000 per year. Even today, Taiwan ranks among the top three countries of origin of foreign graduate students in the United States. In the beginning, as might have been predicted, very few of the students returned to Taiwan after the completion of their studies. From the late 1970s, there began to be a reverse flow, not only amongst the newly graduated, but amongst those who had worked in the United States for years. This is because of both the deteriorating market for scientific and technical personnel in the United States and the increasing opportunities in Taiwan. Today, the overwhelming proportion of the senior executives of firms in the Hsinchiu Science-Based Industrial Park – Taiwan's Silicon Valley – have studied, trained and worked in the United States. The human capital 'hoarded' abroad has proved to be a most important asset for Taiwan as it attempts to upgrade its industries.

Technology in its narrow technical sense must be considered another important factor. Here, the role of multinational corporations, Japanese trading firms, and overseas Chinese businessmen play an important role. The 'Flying Geese' paradigm of technology transfer, with Japan being the leading goose, has some truth. Technology came with foreign direct investment by firms seeking lower production costs as well as circumventing quota restrictions. Taiwan's early industrialisation is essentially characterised by the manufacture of what became too costly to produce first in Japan and then in Hong Kong. And when it became too costly to produce in Taiwan, the production shifted to South Korea, and then to

Southeast Asia, and more recently to mainland China. (This is because expertise – management, technical as well as marketing – is more industry-specific than location-specific, so firms prefer to relocate an existing business rather than start a new separate business.) However, it should be emphasised that during these early years, firms and industries in Taiwan were more in the emulation model than in the innovation mode. Foreign direct investment came to Taiwan not only because of low production costs – there were many countries with even lower production costs. It was partly because of historical and ethnic ties (certainly on the part of the Japanese and overseas Chinese investors). But more importantly, it is because the government in Taiwan adopted an export promotion strategy. This means that the export businesses will be facilitated if not actually favoured. The availability of export earnings in terms of foreign exchange solved one of the most important problems facing foreign investors – how to get the money (original investment and profit) back. A country that does not export, or exports very little, is generally not a good candidate as a host country because potential foreign investors will have to face the transfer problem – the problem of repatriating the original investment and profit. The same argument also applies to potential foreign lenders.

Demand Conditions

The demand conditions that faced Taiwan as it began its process of industrialisation were quite favourable. There was the successful conclusion of the Kennedy round of multilateral trade negotiations, which led to major reductions in tariff and non-tariff trade barriers, and the 1960s and the early 1970s were a period of robust growth in the industrialised countries. As a result, world trade grew very rapidly and Taiwan greatly benefited. Most developing countries at the time were enamoured of the import substitution strategy of economic development, and Taiwan did not have too many competitors on the world market. The 'voluntary export restraints' in textiles accelerated the migration of industries from Japan and Hong Kong to Taiwan.[16]

Related and Supporting Industries

Taiwan's experience provides strong empirical support for the idea that industries tend to grow in clusters. The first wave of industrialisation was based on the processing of agricultural products such as pineapples, asparagus and mushrooms. This was followed by the development of an export-oriented textile industry cluster, including spinning, weaving, dyeing, and garment manufacturing, which soon became the largest exporting industry. The plastics industry was begun in the mid-1950s and soon integrated forward to the production of synthetic fibres and other plastics, and backward to petrochemicals. More recently, the cluster of computer and computer peripheral industries, which has as its origin the manufacture of television sets, has supplanted textiles as the largest exporting industry. In every instance, a cluster of industries developed on the basis of related, but at the same time variegated, capabilities. There were significant knowledge and skill complementarities among industries within the same cluster.

Firm Strategy, Structure, and Rivalry

In most of the export industries, there is no dominant firm. Most of the firms in Taiwan are small – the largest conglomerate in Taiwan is only about one-tenth the size of the largest conglomerate in South Korea. Moreover, the world market is highly competitive, and there is no major product on which Taiwan can enjoy monopolistic rents even though it may have a very large market share. Competition is quite fierce in Taiwan itself, because there is free entry in most industry and industry segments. For example, Taiwan at one time had close to 100 notebook computer manufacturers. The combination of both domestic and international competition keeps the export-oriented firms and industries efficient. And there is very little that the government can do because, while it can protect the domestic market, it cannot influence the world market. As a result, Taiwanese firms have learnt to rely on themselves, rather than government assistance, with one notable exception, and that is in the R&D area, which will be discussed below. It should be noted that most Taiwan firms are still family firms and effectively owner-managed. There is thus no incentive incompatibility problem – the interests of the owner and the manager are identical. This is probably one reason why Taiwanese firms have been able to respond and adjust quickly to changing competitive advantage.

Geographical and Industrial Concentration

Taiwan is basically a very small country. One can drive from the northern end to the southern end in a few hours. However, the geographical proximity of Taiwan to Japan and Hong Kong might have been important in its early development. It is probably not entirely accidental that almost all of the successful developing countries are in East Asia. There is a neighbourhood effect: and the 'flying geese' are all geographically close to one another.

The Role of Government

The government of Taiwan played a very important role in its economic development. First and foremost, it provided an environment of macro-economic stability – there were budget surpluses, low inflation (except during the two oil crises) and mostly positive real rates of interest – which in turn encouraged both savings and investment. These policies helped to ensure a more equitable distribution of income.[17] The exchange rate was kept quite stable for most of the period – between 1960 and 1986, it varied only within a ten per cent band. The government used tax and other incentives to promote industrial investment. Second, the government very early on decided to rely on the private sector, rather than the public, to spearhead its development efforts. It maintained an efficient civil service, simplified red tape and generally allowed free entry, especially in the export-oriented industries. The government tried to promote competition whenever it could. For example, in most countries the textile export quotas are regarded as the properties of the firms who were initially allocated the quotas. Many firms simply 'rented' out their quotas to other firms and collected their 'rent'. Taiwan devised a system in which firms could only retain 80 per cent of their previous year's quota, each year; the quota released would be reallocated to firms whose export orders have the highest unit value for that category. This way, it is possible for a new firm to enter the business. Third, the government adopted an export promotion strategy after an initial short phase of import substitution. An export-oriented strategy (as opposed to an import substitution strategy) left very little room for rent-seeking because of competition in the world market that is outside the control of the home government. As a result, the export-oriented firms and industries must be efficient and create real value in order to survive. An export-oriented strategy also facilitated technology transfer through foreign direct investment, as discussed above. Fourth, the government built up the domestic infrastructure, including not only airports, highways, ports, railroads, and electric utilities, but also housing for low-income families and industrial estates and zones. It established the first Export Processing Zone in the world, in Kaohsiung, which was widely emulated. It set up the Hsinchu Science-Based Industrial Park, a clone of the Silicon Valley, in 1983, which has become the home of high-technology firms in Taiwan. The state extended universal education and invested heavily first in schools, then in colleges and universities. In the 1970s the state which had hithertofore largely eschewed an industrial policy set up a number of research institutes and dramatically increased its funding of large-scale industrial R&D projects. A primary centre of industrial R&D is the Industrial Technology Research Institute, which has been reponsible for initiating or reviving several major industries, including bicycles, sporting goods, computers and computer peripherals, and semiconductors.

The personal computer industry in Taiwan provides a case of successful government-financed R&D. In the early 1980s, the personal computer industries in Taiwan and Hong Kong consisted mostly of 'pirates' who simply copied foreign designs without licence or royalty. All that activity was stopped as a result of legal action on the part of the US and other computer manufacturers. Then the Industrial Technology Research Institute came along and developed it own BIOS chip which enabled the personal computer industry in Taiwan to continue to develop (with foreign licence, of course). In Hong Kong the personal computer industry, lacking the R&D effort, never recovered. The Industrial Technology Research Institute also developed the notebook computer for a consortium of manufacturers in Taiwan. Government support for R&D is quite essential given Taiwan's particular industrial structure, which consists of a large number of diverse but relatively small firms. The advantages of this mode of industrialisation are the equitable distribution of income, the ease of entry and exit, the flexibility and the social mobility. The disadvantage is that there are few firms large enough and financially strong enough to undertake long-term and high-risk investments, especially in R&D. The state has to play a leading role in the support of R&D and sometimes even in the establishment of new industries. For example, public investment was instrumental in the establishment of China Steel and the semiconductor industries because there was insufficient interest in the private sector. The successful public enterprises are, as a rule, privatised once they are able to stand on their own. Even though Taiwan's R&D expenditure as a percentage of GNP has been rising over time, it is still low – about 1.7 in 1990 – in comparison with the industrialised countries and also in comparison with South Korea. This is an area where additional resources are required to offset the diminishing marginal productivity of physical capital if Taiwan is to maintain its competitive advantage in the future. Finally the government of Taiwan has so far also managed to avoid the welfare state syndrome, preserving the incentives for individuals to work, save and invest. This helped to lower the cost of doing business and avoid a huge government budget deficit. But as Taiwan progresses to the 'wealth-driven' phase, the social welfare agenda may be hard to avoid.

The Role of Chance

Chance plays a not insignificant role in Taiwan's development. After the defeated Nationalist Government fled to Taiwan in 1949, without an ally and without any foreign aid, the US withdrew its support totally. The sudden outbreak of the Korean War changed the whole picture. Because of its important strategic location and the perceived need to contain an expansionist mainland China, US military and economic aid to Taiwan soon resumed and a mutual defence treaty was concluded beween the Republic of China on Taiwan and the United States. Without US aid, it is not certain whether Taiwan would have survived as an independent entity. The Cold War and the Korean War also changed the perspective of US policy makers on Japan. The original intention of keeping Japan as a mostly agricultural country gave way to the notion of building up Japan's economy as a bulwark against communism. The success of the land reform in Taiwan in the 1950s laid the foundation for the subsequent increase in agricultural productivity, which in turn allowed labour and resources to be transferred to support the development of the industrial sector.[18] It was critical; but it is only one of at most a handful of successful land reforms in the world. The decision by the government to rely on the private sector was not pre-ordained and could have gone the other way. One might mention the expansion of world trade as a result of the Kennedy round and the transportation and communication revolution, which greatly facilitated the growth of export firms and industries in Taiwan. The imposition of textile quotas by the industrialised countries on Japan and Hong Kong had a favourable impact – it diverted investment and trade to Taiwan. There were many elements of chance and pure luck. Yes, Taiwan was lucky. However, Taiwan was able to capitalise on the opportunities that materialised. Perhaps the ability to capitalise on opportunities is itself an important source of competitive advantage.

5. CONCLUDING REMARKS

In terms of Porter's 'Four-Phase' paradigm (see Introduction), Taiwan probably progressed from factor- or labour-driven to investment-driven some time in the mid to late 1960s, when surplus labour began to run out. It is just now beginning to enter the 'innovation-driven' phase.[19] Taiwan is still quite a distance from being 'wealth-driven', but the current fixation of its citizens with asset market speculation and the rapidly expanding social welfare agenda are early warning signals that the wealth-driven phase may actually not be so far away. Nevertheless, Taiwan's rising labour productivity and export shares since the early 1960s, both in the aggregate and in selected industry and industry segments, provide strong empirical evidence that it has been able to enhance and maintain its competitive advantage, in Porter's sense, over time.

What can we learn about 'competitive advantage' from the experience of Taiwan? We have seen that Taiwan has had to undergo rapid and continuous transformation of its industrial capabilities during the last three decades. Starting from a narrow export base consisting principally of bananas and sugar, it progressed through a variety of products (for example textiles, garments, shoes, umbrellas, home appliances, television sets, printed circuit boards and bicycles). It now includes amongst its exports machine tools, microcomputers, and semiconductors (of submicron fineness). Computers and computer perhipherals have become its most important export industry. Taiwan's experience shows that competitive advantage is ephemeral and fleeting, and that firms must work constantly to maintain an existing competitive advantage, or to create and exploit a competitive advantage that has not existed before. In the process, many Taiwan firms have come and gone. Countries with real natural resource wealth and large protectable domestic markets can afford not to try as hard; but for Taiwan, a small country with a population of 20 million and hence a limited domestic market and no natural resources, maintenance of competitiveness in international trade is essential for the improvement and even maintenance of its standard of living. Taiwan's experience also shows convincingly that it is possible for a country to maintain a competitive advantage in an evolving group of industries over time, even in the face of an appreciating exchange rate. It also shows that industrial and technological capabilities indeed develop around clusters of related industries, or industry segments, and that there is a progression of industries, sometimes not so orderly, along the technological scale. Emulation, learning by doing, technology transfer, as well as indigenous R&D all play a role in this progression. Taiwan's experience confirms that know-how and skills are more industry-specific than location-specific, and that is the reason firms are more likely to relocate their factories abroad when they lose comparative or competitive advantage than to undertake a new venture in a different industry in the home country. What were some of the factors that made it possible for Taiwan to acquire and maintan its competitive advantage? What did Taiwan have or do that other, less successful, developing countries did not?[20]

First, the high national savings ratio of Taiwan implies the ready availability of domestic investment funds that makes possible the rapid transformation of industries to accommodate the shifting winds of export demand and comparative/competitive advantage. Second, Taiwan has been well served by a sound and far-sighted educational policy. The considerable human capital embodied in its citizens or former citizens that reside abroad can be readily tapped if needed. Third the export orientation has proved to be a great assistance. International competition in the world market puts enormous pressure on firms to perform. There is not too much rent-seeking opportunity in export industries. The export firms and industries must be efficient to survive. The non-tradable sector of Taiwan, especially in the public works sector, is, by contrast, a model of inefficiency and low productivity. Taiwan has the distinction of building the world's most expensive, and by all accounts, nowhere near the best, yet to be completed mass transit system per kilometre. In terms of efficiency, Taiwan is basically a dual economy – efficient in the tradable sector and inefficient in the non-tradable sector. Free from external competitive pressure, there is little incentive for firms in the non-tradable sector to be efficient, especially when collusion is relatively easy. Fourth, another favourable factor is the industrial structure which consists mostly of small firms. The ability to learn and adapt quickly to changing market conditions is a competitive advantage. Small firms are too small to attempt to protect a vested interest or to lobby for a government handout. Small firms tend to have a sharper competitive edge. The disadvantages of an industrial structure dominated by small firms are: first, lumpy investments with long-term payoffs will not be undertaken; and, second, high-risk investments, such as R&D, will not be undertaken, not only because the payoffs are long in coming but also because of the inability to pool and share risks. Fifth, the government played an extremely important role in Taiwan. It promoted the appropriate education and undertook long-term, high-risk investments, including R&D. Taiwan's experience illustrates that the type of industrial structure determines the proper role of the government and vice versa.

One can reinterpret 'competitive advantage' as a dynamic version of comparative advantage, provided that one recognises that:

(1) there are many factors of production beyond the customary capital labour, land and natural resources; and
(2) the factors of production are not necessarily 'natural' and can be created, enhanced, depleted and lost.

The other factors of production may include human capital, knowledge, skills, patents, and know-how. There may be 'higher-order comparative advantages' beyond the customary ones. The production functions, in terms of only the traditional factors of capital and labour, are in fact different across countries because of the presence of these other factors. Natural resource endowment and human capital (skill accumulation) may actually be substitutes rather than complements in production.[21] Countries without many natural resources must invest more in these other factors, such as human capital, in order to have a competitive advantage. Unlike static comparative advantage based on natural resources, competitive advantage must be constantly improved and upgraded. Competitive advantage can be created or lost, or competed away through invention, innovation and sometimes depletion. Japan maintains its competitive advantage by constantly renovating its capital stock and by investing heavily in R&D activities. Edward Leamer presented empirical evidence that international trade flows are determined by 'resources' that are not necessarily 'natural', that is, resources that can be created such as human capital and knowledge or R&D capital.[22] Building on Leamer's work, Li-Gang Song investigated the relationship between international trade and resource abundance, using newly assembled data from many developed and developing countries, and found that the international trade flows in ten aggregate commodity groups are well explained by 11 types of resource endowments.[23] These resource endowments go beyond the traditional primary inputs of capital, labour and land and include human capital as well as technology inputs, which, like capital, can be created. The usual theory of comparative advantage, based on resource endowments, is thereby extended and given a new meaning.

Given the rapid turnover of industry-level, not to mention firm-level, competitive advantage, it may perhaps be more interesting and useful to focus on the changes in competitive advantage over time and the process by which industry-level competitive advantage passes from one country to another. One can typically see a pattern – as the export share declines in one country, it begins to rise in another country – replicating itself over many countries and over time. A worthy research project is to identify the determinants of the country and time sequences. Finally, while the theory of comparative advantage can be used to explain international trade flows, it is not able to explain the distribution of the gains from trade between two trading countries, or their terms of trade. The theory of competitive advantage may be more promising for explaining the distribution of gains from trade, because relative competitive advantage can be expected to determine the relative bargaining power of the trading partners. The theory will need to focus on the value-added (which has an impact on the amount of income generated and the distribution of rent)[24] in addition to the gross value of trade. And while the distribution of gains from trade cannot be easily predicted by the theory of comparative advantage, it can clearly be affected by strategies used by the firms. For example, the critical components strategy is used by many Japanese firms. Under this strategy, a critical, and usually technically sophisticated, component of a product is priced at a level so high that most of the profit is captured by the manufacturers of the critical component rather than the manufacturer of the product. For example, Japan was a leading manufacturer of cameras. As the cost of production rose in Japan relative to other East Asian countries, the manufacture or assembly of cameras has been mostly relocated to low-cost countries. However, Japan maintains the production of the plastic lens, a critical component of the camera. By maintaining a very high price for the plastic lens, the Japanese manufacturers effectively appropriate most of the profits in the manufacture of cameras. As long as there are no alternative sources of supply of the plastic lens, the manufacturers of cameras will have to continue to pay the high prices. They, in effect, have very little competitive advantage relative to the manufacturers of the plastic lens, even if their export shares of the world market are very high. Other examples of critical components include the liquid crystal displays for notebook computers and the heads for video-camera recorders. Taiwan's experience suggests that competitive advantage for small developing countries may be very different because of the general lack of market power. Competitive advantage depends on the creation or discovery of market niches in which the firm or industry can excel. In the long run, competitive advantage can be sustained only through continuous innovation. Since capital is increasingly more mobile, availability of domestic capital is no longer a large advantage. Long-term optimism for Taiwan is based on its human resources. Taiwan has a sound educational system with a great deal of depth and breadth, which makes it relatively easy to develop skills complementary to new technologies. The long gestation period of investment in human capital now works in Taiwan's advantage, because while it took a long time for Taiwan to build up its human capital, it will also take a potential competitor a long time to catch up. Taiwan has the additional advantage of being able to tap into the large number of its former residents now working in scientific and technical capabilities in the industrialised countries. In order to attract, and keep, this latter group of people, who are also very mobile, the government must strive to maintain an economic, political and social environment that provides the incentives for innovation. It must delay, as much as possible, its entry into the 'wealth-driven' phase.

NOTES

1. M.E. Porter, *The Competitive Advantage of Nations* (New York, 1990), p.25.
2. There are measures of the number of patents that take into account and give greater weight to the degree of relatedness of the patents.
3. The substantial shares may not necessarily be sustained in individual industries.
4. Tatung has made an effort in audio and video electronics but is not yet a household name.
5. World Bank, *The East Asian Miracle: Economic Growth and Public Policy* (Oxford, 1993).
6. GNP per capita data are taken from the Council for Economic Planning and Development, *Taiwan Statistical Data Book, 1992* (Taipei, 1992), pp.25, 30. Exchange rates used are the annual averages of the buying and selling rates (ibid., p.152).
7. Taiwan's 'take-off' into sustained economic growth may be dated from 1962. See J.I. Kim and L.J. Lau, 'The Sources of Economic Growth in the East Asian Newly Industrialised Countries', *Journal of the Japanese and International Economies*, forthcoming.
8. M. Abramovitz and P.A. David, 'Reinterpreting Economic Growth: Parables and Realities' *American Economic Review* Vol.63, (1973), p.431, table 2.
9. IMF, *International Financial Statistics Yearbook* (Washington, various issues).
10. Human capital is measured as the number of years of formal education per person of the working population, defined as persons between the ages of 15 and 64 inclusive.
11. J.I. Kim and L.J. Lau, 'The Role of Human Capital in the Economic Growth of the East Asian Newly Industrialised Countries', paper presented at the Allied Social Science Associations Meeting, January 1994.
12. Kim and Lau, 'Sources of Economic Growth . . .', and discussion in section 4 below. The same result was found earlier in L.J. Lau (ed.), *Models of Development: A Comparative Study of Economic Growth in South Korea and Taiwan* (San Francisco, 1990), pp.183–215, using the more traditional growth of total factor productivity formula.
13. Kim and Lau, 'The role of human capital . . .'.
14. Ibid.
15. See P.K.C. Liu, 'Science, Technology and Human Capital Formation', in G. Ranis (ed.), *Taiwan: From Developing to Mature Economy* (Boulder, 1992), pp.357–91.
16. The 'voluntary export restraints' on textiles also helped South Korea, as did the subsequent Japanese 'voluntary export restraint' an automobile exports to the United States.
17. The 'agriculture first' strategy, which was implemented in the early 1950s, laid the foundations for the subsequent development and growth.
18. The success of land reform was partly helped by the fact that it was carried out mostly by people who did not own any land and hence had no vested interest in the status quo.
19. One should bear in mind that 'innovation' is always understood to be relative to the home country.

20. Some would argue that it was the pressure caused by the military threat of mainland China (as South Korea was similarly threatened by North Korea) that spurred the people of Taiwan to extra efforts.
21. It is possible that an abundant natural resource endowment may diminish the incentive to acquire human capital (education, knowledge, skill) in the same way that a person with inherited wealth may decide that it is not worthwhile to acquire additional human capital.
22. E.E. Leamer, *Source of International Comparative Advantage: Theory and Evidence* (Camb. Mass., 1984).
23. L.G. Song, 'Sources of International Comparative Advantage: Further Evidence' (Ph.D.: Australian National University, 1993).
24. Transfer pricing issues may also be involved if the trade was conducted between affiliated businesses, such as a parent firm and its foreign subsidiary.